# CLARA *and* ME

DEANNA KAWATSKI

# CLARA *and* ME

*T*he Story of
an Unexpected
Friendship

WHITECAP BOOKS
VANCOUVER/TORONTO

Edited by Carolyn Bateman
Cover design by Val Speidel
Cover photo by Paul Bailey; inset photograph by Natalia Kawatski
Interior design by Warren Clark
Typeset by Warren Clark

Printed and bound in Canada.

**Canadian Cataloguing in Publication Data**

Kawatski, Deanna, 1951–
    Clara and me

    ISBN 1-55110-489-X

    1. Kawatski, Deanna, 1951– 2. British Columbia, Northern—Biogra-
phy. 3. Frontier and pioneer life—British Columbia, Northern. 4. Mentally
handicapped—British Columbia, Northern—Biography. I. Title.
FC3845. N67Z49 1996       971.1'8504'092       C96-910370-0
F1089.5.N87K38 1996

The publisher acknowledges the support of the Canada Council and the
Cultural Services Branch of the Government of British Columbia in making
this publication possible.

*Dedicated to*
*the diversity that deepens*
*our world and all the souls*
*who have been shunned.*

# Contents

# Acknowledgements

My thanks move in the following directions:

To Clara Handel for her warm friendship.

To my mother, Lorna Barnhardt, who listened while I read aloud each completed chapter.

To my twin sister, Donna Trent, with whom I first learned to share.

To Natalia and Ben-Kyle, who accept the faraway look I get when writing a book.

To Eric Procunier for his love and support, and for starting the fire.

To Fritz Handel for his friendship and encouragement to tell this story.

To Joyce Dunn for her warmth and words of praise.

To Tommy Walker for the account of his adventures in Spatsizi and for helping it to become a park.

To my editor, Carolyn Bateman, for the wise perceptions and gentle suggestions that guided me through the final stages of writing *Clara and Me*.

To the wilderness that cradled me all those years and inspired me with its immense power and beauty.

Above all I thank the Divine.

ᏇᏇᏇᏇ

# *Prologue*

I was born with a built-in companion, a twin sister who, we joked, insisted I emerge first into the April morning in Salmon Arm, British Columbia. It was 1951. Our great-grandmother and her third husband had been among the first white settlers in the North Shuswap region, and our mother had grown up there as well.

As small children we padded barefoot along the smooth dirt road. The sight of a squashed garter snake, its guts obscene beside a puddle, would bring us to an abrupt halt, our toes recoiling in abhorrence. Then white-footed we'd flee across the pasture, dodging cowpies in our flight. Never could I get my fill of hiking. Ever eager to see what was around the elusive next corner, I would lure a less-than-keen sister with me. Donna would draw to a stiff halt at the first hill and declare her walk done. For eighteen years we moved as a single unit even though we were opposite in many ways. I was a bookworm, a class librarian by grade 3. Sprawled on our grandmother's front porch, where a maverick wind spurred the Virginia creeper to dance, was one of my favourite places on earth. The frenzy of leaf shadow on the pages of *Robinson Crusoe, Little Women,* or *What Katy Did* would draw me back to the present, where Donna tapped her foot, waiting for me to emerge from my trance. Donna hated to read, and when a letter arrived, and they were often addressed to both of us, I would devour it quickly and offer it to her. "How long is it?" was her predictable plea.

When we were three years old and our brother Tom was six, our father drowned in Shuswap Lake. Three years later we were forced to leave our home and move to the Agricultural Research Station outside Kamloops, where our mother gained secretarial work. Our grandmother lived with us from that point on and helped to raise us. Despite my longing for the lake, this move also meant a whole new world to explore. Oblivious to the bushes, spring-loaded with rattlesnakes, we'd romp the tumbleweed hills for hours, our feet evading spiky clumps of cacti, my head lost in sage-steeped dreams. Later we moved into Kamloops, but I lived for the summers when we could return to Shuswap Lake. After high school I migrated to Vancouver where I attended UBC (I quit in my second year) while Donna remained in Kamloops working as a telephone operator. Our parting was traumatic, and the tight twin bond left us with a permanent longing for a sidekick, a shadow self. It was as though we were each one half of a whole person.

In 1971, my feet itching with wanderlust, I stepped onto a jumbo jet for the first of what would amount to ten crossings of the Atlantic Ocean in the next eight years. In broken-down sandals, I wandered from western Europe to India and back again. My feet played a symphony on foreign streets, languid beaches, and wondering hills, finding with relief the green park-heart throbbing at the centre of each whirlpool of traffic and silently desperate crowds. Lured on by the dream of what lay just beyond the next bend, I composed poetry to the steady beat of boots on the earth drum.

At age twenty-three I moved to Paris forever and lasted three months. Restlessly I wandered the banks and bridges of the Seine and also spent hours sitting in cafés, scribbling away on my first novel.

My passion for writing began as a small child. I excelled at composition and composed poetry in my spare time. As I roamed I kept a journal. It was also in Paris that my feet first stepped inside a studio and discovered the joy of dance. For the next five years, it became my main passion apart from writing, a solid radiant ribbon woven through my wandering.

It was financial realities that brought my feet back to earth with rhythmic regularity, and sooner or later I would find myself clambering through a Canadian clear-cut, smeared with soot from slash-burning, a mattock clutched in one torn glove. Surrounded by an aura of bug dope and mosquitoes, I methodically stomped the earth beside the tender seedlings, planting trees for tomorrow.

With my tomorrow bought and paid for, my feet would leave the earth again to roam the far side of the globe. Spain, Morocco, Italy, Israel, Greece, and Yugoslavia all felt, then promptly forgot, the tempo of my passing.

As the years wore on, travelling lost its lustre and took on a sameness. Increasingly I found myself longing for a home and children. In 1978, fresh from Israel and Italy, I was lucky enough to land a job as lookout attendant for the B.C. Forest Service. I flew from Shuswap Lake to the northern town of Stewart, then 120 miles further north, to the Bob Quinn fire tower.

When the chopper dropped me, my dog, and my gear off on the mountaintop, Jay Kawatski had been living in the region as a hermit for five and a half years. When he heard that, for the first time, a woman was stationed on the mountain, he journeyed by canoe and on foot a distance of ten miles to visit.

Jay arrived dressed in a mink and otter cape and marten hat, with his blond hair and beard well groomed. In a neighbourly fashion, he drew gifts from his well-worn pack. These included pale green Araucana eggs, succulent carrots, and 'Blue Mountain' potatoes the colour of amethysts. These marvels may well have been coming from

Middle Earth. I had never seen purple potatoes before, and the fact that they had been grown in the wilderness more than one hundred miles from established farms and fields made them all the more intriguing.

Our friendship developed into a romance. Having grown up in a family of fourteen on a small farm in Wisconsin, Jay also dreamed of sharing his life. The next summer when I returned to the lookout, he presented me with a moose antler engagement ring and I accepted. I was of pioneer stock myself and I yearned to settle in a wild place. In the fall of 1979, we were married at Shuswap Lake.

In 1980, Natalia was born three miles from the present site of the homestead in Jay's first cabin beside Desiré Lake. We had wanted a homebirth, and Jay was prepared to help me through the night-long labour. Even then our garden site was in the Ningunsaw Valley. Natalia's due date came and went, and we knew that our garden was in desperate need of water, so we decided to hike down and tend it. Ironically, I went into labour there. To get back to the lake I had to endure a torturous three-mile hike through a blizzard of bugs. For strength I focussed on a strong pine outside the window during labour. Finally, on June 20, with the first light of day glowing on the mountains, and to the tune of a wildly yodelling loon couple on the lake, Natalia entered the world.

Ben was due in winter five years later, and I thought it best to travel 120 miles to the nearest town of Stewart so the baby could be delivered by a doctor. Ironically, baby Ben arrived during the only eight-hour period when there wasn't a doctor in town.

We had built our log home on a bench of land overlooking our flat, fertile, semi-shaded garden. Across the clearing wandered Natty Creek, and in planning the layout of our garden we had simply attached our plots to its meanderings. Surrounding us was graceful virgin forest. The ground was covered with a plush carpet of moss that concealed a maze of fallen trees. At chest height grew a profusion of plants including red elderberry and thorn-brandishing devil's club. Higher still beckoned an abundance of lichen-hung alder. Above all this, towering spruce, balsam fir, and cottonwood reduced us to the size of elves.

We all pitched in to help with what had grown from a fifty-by-one-hundred-foot plot to nearly three acres. Our goal was freedom from the system, and after more than a decade of dedication we had become at least 75 percent self-sufficient in food. Sometimes an outing to a nearby lake or mountaintop would have to be sacrificed for the sake of harvesting the dead-ripe raspberries, or peas on the verge of overmaturity. Breaks from the constant round of chores were rare and frequently ephemeral.

There was no road access to our homestead, and it was a three-mile hike over a rough, bog-riddled foot trail to get to the gravel highway, which in turn was 120 miles from town. Apart from the small and transient population at the highways camp, five miles away, no one lived for more than one hundred miles in most directions.

Our annual income didn't exceed five thousand dollars, and most of it came from Jay's woodcarvings, taxidermy, and snowshoe making, by my magazine articles, and by keeping weather records for the Atmospheric Environmental Service.

We had begun by squatting on the land, but after locking horns with the government we were granted a License of Occupation and were required to pay taxes. To save money, we visited dumps when we could and recycled whatever caught the eye.

Overall we were happy to wear hand-me-downs. Natalia wasn't concerned about a fancy wardrobe for school, since school was the homemade desk and blackboard in our living room. It took her two hours a day to achieve top marks through the government correspondence system. Despite her enthusiasm for the life into which she had been born, I sensed how much my daughter yearned for regular contact with children her own age.

I had continued to write, and *Bird, Bubble and Stream,* a collection of poetry, was published by Fiddlehead Press in 1980, the same year that "Lookout Life," my first magazine article, appeared in *Westworld.* For the next six years I continued to scribble when I had the chance, but I submitted only sporadically, and, as in the past, stuffed most of the material away in boxes. Then, in 1986, *Outdoor Canada* bought "At Home with the Cliff Dwellers," the story of a day Jay and I spent in the company of a band of Rocky Mountain goats. This was followed by another assignment from *Outdoor Canada* and a simultaneous request from *Harrowsmith.* The stories, both about our lifestyle, appeared on the newsstands in 1987 within two weeks of each other. I continued to get further work with *Harrowsmith,* then later *B.C. Woman to Woman, Country Woman,* and *Mother Earth News.*

It was evident from letters I received from all over the United States and as far away as Wales and Costa Rica that many thought we were leading the ideal life. But most often these enthusiasts were men, and their idealized rant about how they imagined life beyond the rat race ended on a common note. *My wife says if I leave town and move to the bush, I'm on my own.*

My stories had also attracted visitors, including the three German men who were still with us in the autumn of 1989. In order to experience the wilderness and also to learn skills of self-reliance, they had ventured to our far-flung valley from Berlin. Since the previous May, Jay had helped them construct a snug log cabin and it was only a few days away from completion. Recently our house had been transformed into something akin to a snowshoe-building school. While Philipp, Roy, and Christoph leaned close, Jay deftly showed them how to weave the murky moosehide lacing onto the birch frames with a moose antler needle. Dried and varnished, the homemade webbing took on an amber translucence, and numerous completed pairs swung like pendulums beneath the stairs.

As much as I enjoyed the company of these visitors, I kept wishing there were more women and children among them. And more often than not, on holiday from what they considered to be the real world of concrete and clock time, they failed to grasp the full extent of the work involved simply in surviving so far from civilization. Nervous at the prospect of isolation, the Germans had brought a radio-phone with them, and for the first time in ten years, we had sporadic communication with the outside world. Sporadic because most of the time it didn't work. I was so thankful that my mother made an annual visit, driving a thousand miles north to see us, sometimes with others, and often on her own. With six days of travel involved, she couldn't stay more than four days. My brother and his family made a single visit, and my sister and her family came several times, including one critically cold Christmas.

There were many blissful moments, but as the years wore on the happy times shared with Jay became fewer and farther between. The isolation magnified our difficulties, fostered extreme positions, and I hung onto the hurt far past the point of healthy. Even so, our lifestyle embodied all the elements I had searched so long to find. I no longer imagined life beyond the Ningunsaw Valley. I wanted nothing more or less. Except a female neighbour.

# Meeting Clara

With our eyes clenched shut, my two children and I stood with our backs to the galloping green water and clutched our chosen wishing rocks. On either side of the Ningunsaw River, beyond the sand scattered with round grey rocks and tiny seedlings, birch and cottonwood trembled with the glory of autumn. Above the golden blaze, and seamed with the tumble of creeks through crimson brush, soared the Coast Mountains. The silhouette of snowy peaks was sharpened by an ultramarine sky.

I caught the flutter of Natalia's eyelids as she struggled to concentrate on her wish. Born and raised in the bush, at age nine Natalia was an intensely creative and somewhat serious child. Her thick, ginger-coloured ponytail, which had been captured squarely on top of her head that morning, had now slipped to one side. Despite the October chill in the air, she had stripped off her socks and shoes and now wriggled her toes in the fine black sand, imprinted with fresh moose tracks. I didn't ask Natalia what her wish was and she didn't ask about mine. We both believed that the telling would render them infertile.

Blond Ben, whose warm brown eyes were lost behind quivering lids, wasn't quite four years old and had less than perfect aim. Natalia and I both backed away before he flung his rock, which landed far downstream of its intended mark.

Wishes cast, we plunked down together on a silver cottonwood log, and, while the kids munched apples, I read aloud from *The Golly Sisters Go West*. The rise and fall of their laughter was swallowed by the riot of river voices.

What I had wished for, in fact what I longed for most in the remote valley in which we homesteaded, was a female neighbour. For eleven years I had dreamed of having another woman within walking distance. Especially as a mother of young children, I felt acutely at times the need for contact with other women. I longed for the support that could come from the wisdom of experience, the female voice of reassurance saying, yes I've been there, it's perfectly natural, don't give up, you'll get through it, it will be okay. My women friends, who I saw only sporadically, leaned heavily on one another for support through various forms of strife, even claiming that they wouldn't be able to survive without talking to one another. In many cases these conversations took place on a daily basis.

But the longing didn't arise solely out of desperation. It also stemmed from a deep tradition of sharing special events and rituals with other women, ceremonies that gave life an added dimension of meaning. Besides, I had grown up in a matriarchy, and all my life I had related most comfortably to other women. There was a unique flow that happened not only because we shared physical characteristics, but also because we inhabited some of the same psychic territory.

Our extreme isolation sometimes stirred within me an intense craving for a social life. In daydreams born of loneliness, I imagined the ideal woman next door. Like me she would be in her late thirties and would not only be intelligent, and an avid outdoorswoman who loved to hike and revel in the natural world, she would also be passionately literary and creative. We would engage in enriching conversation and would share not just numerous facets of child raising, gardening, and crafts but at last I would be able to share books, passages, favourite quotes.

Often, in a kind of delirium, I would plan parties, dinners, outings with my phantom neighbour. On a bright day we could pack a picnic and a good book and take our children—ideally she would have two as well—upstream as far as the narrow canyon in the Ningunsaw River. Everyone would listen spellbound as I read aloud, and then the children would play while my ghost friend and I leaned back in the sunshine and enjoyed a break from domestic drudgery.

I would present her with gifts of homemade huckleberry jelly and rabbit skin moccasins for her children and she would give me perfume made from wild roses. It would be a friendship that would last our whole lives. How could I know that, in October 1989, fate waited just ahead eager to make a mockery of my vision?

Did I dare to dream that this mythical woman may also read my own literary attempts and offer constructive feedback? Even praise? As a scribe in isolation I often craved contact with the writing community. I truly was a voice in the wilderness and the simple act of mailing a story was a feat in itself. It began with a three-mile hike over a bog-riddled trail, with lung-tugging inclines, tree-crowded turns, and the ever present possibility of confronting bears, wolves, or even wolverines. This was followed by the risky business of hitchhiking 120 miles south to the tiny town of Stewart. In my mud-spattered gumboots, with the straps of my packsack biting into my shoulders, and wearing a somewhat bushed expression, I would burst through the door of a post office that was itself not much bigger than an envelope. More than once, distant magazines such as *Mother Earth News* based in New York City had used their urban strategies to reach me quickly. Their couriered dispatches in their bright blue, eagle-embellished envelopes inevitably lay there for a month or more.

With thoughts of all the work at home tugging at my sleeve and whines of protest from Natalia and Ben, we left the river and headed north through the woods. Five minutes later, as the kids fought for first place on the trail, our handmade house came into view. Our black terrier, Spooky, who had been somehow left behind, came dashing down to meet us.

Blond-bearded Jay waved from the front porch where he sat on a bench washing out rabbit skins. Behind him, the front of what had grown over the years into an elaborate log home was lush with large bundles of homegrown wheat, hung beneath the eaves to dry. Miraculously, in a region where rain could descend for weeks, we had managed to grow grain. I felt a sense of security as I gazed at the wheat. After all, wasn't the ability to produce our own bread from scratch the ultimate in self-sufficiency? Accompanying this was a surge of pride in my husband, who performed every job with exceptional skill and efficiency. As we drew closer, I called up, "How's it going?" but he didn't appear to hear. Possibly the creek had drowned out my voice. With head bent to the task at hand, Jay worked the skins in a silent and sullen manner. He never seemed to take a break, not even a simple outing to the river with the children and me. As the years wore on, I felt more and more of a need for his companionship. However, Jay was aware of our fast approaching wedding anniversary, and with each new remark he made about the possibility of celebrating it, my spirits rose.

On October 19, our German guests Philipp and Roy cheerfully offered to look after Natalia and Ben, giving Jay and I a rare chance to go out as a couple. The day bore dual significance. Not only did it mark the tenth anniversary of what had turned out to be, at times, a troubled marriage. It was also the first time I met Clara.

Flipping the tail of his coonskin cap out from under the collar of his heavy wool hunting jacket, and with an extra reminder to the two men to keep their eyes on the woodstoves, long-legged Jay was off like a shot. Pressed for time, as always with my high-energy husband,

I cut my primping short, then snatched a coat off the hook, mittens off the shelf, and sped down the path behind him. The first snow of the season was sprinkled with spruce needles on top of a light embroidery of mouse and squirrel tracks. Sidestepping bog holes with fragile lids of ice and barkless logs gleaming with the invitation to slip, I toiled after him. Three miles later we arrived at the trailhead and hopped into Josephine, Philipp and Roy's road-beaten pickup truck.

There was still no mention of where we were going as Jay steered north up the lonely Stewart-Cassiar Highway beneath a pale white sky. Under his coonskin cap he was subdued.

Our first stop was five miles north at the local dump. As we wheeled in, a flock of twelve ravens sailed up into the surrounding spruce and balsam trees. Since Jay had yanked off his clammy gumboots and pulled his bedroom slippers on for driving, he stayed behind in the truck.

I hesitantly emerged, pulling my coat closed over my clean mauve sweater and matching corduroy pants. To mark the special occasion, and because bug season was over, I even wore a dab of White Shoulders perfume behind each ear. Two Steller's jays flew from their perch of twisted aluminum siding to the top of a paint can, squawking loudly. Reluctantly I tiptoed through the putrid conglomeration of mouldy food thrown out by mining and logging camps, tin, plastic, shattered glass, and oil. Seizing a potential chicken feed bucket, I stood considering it while Jay rolled down the window and called out that he had handles at home. I took it with me.

Back on the road, I buried myself in an Annie Dillard story called "Ship in a Bottle," featured in an old issue of *Harper's*. Farther north I glanced up. The glacier-webbed mountains were loosening their hold on the landscape, giving way to broader valleys. Grizzly-haunted ridges bordering a hundred-thousand-acre monster called the Iskut burn were highlighted with snow. The huge forest fire, which had been started by lightning, had raged more than thirty years earlier.

As we drove through Iskut Village with its school, Co-op store, and smattering of similar houses, a full sixty-five miles from home, there was still no word of our destination. I didn't ask. As the boreal forest flew by I was gaining a strong sense that Jay's heart was not in this excursion.

Just north of the village, Jay swung west and followed a narrow dirt road to a gravel parking area. Emerging, we crossed a lazy creek by way of a footbridge and followed a trail that wound up a hill beneath a high canopy of pine, to a log house owned by acquaintances named Jim and Irma. The forest floor was moss with a profusion of Labrador tea and kinnikinnick. But the husky that barked from where it was tethered to a tree was the only one at home.

As we retreated across the bridge, I was brought to an abrupt halt by what sounded like babies crying. Then in a flash I recognized the sound. Trumpeter swans! Little Iskut Lake lay just north, and as we stood above the stream, seven swans sailed around in a white and silver circle, as strong and as elegant as ballerinas. My heart was full of gratitude for the gift of this sight on such a special day. I watched them long and hard. Then, snapped from my trance by the sound of an engine, I dashed to the truck.

A short distance south we swung off the gravel highway again and followed a dirt lane to what was our true destination. Quickly we were engulfed by what could only be described as a junk dealer's paradise. As I gazed incredulously at the tangled mound, I began to recognize limbs of the larger anatomy. Trucks and cars without tires or windshields littered the yard while wrecked snowmobiles and their parts mingled with bicycle carcasses and castoff washing machines. Even though this yard lay directly across the road from a native village, the contents belonged to a tall reserved white man named Fritz Handel.

Fritz was outside when we pulled up. With his electric drill rigged up to his solar panels, he was busy working at the back of a native fellow's pickup truck. Fritz had dark receding hair, a scruffy beard, and wise yet wary eyes set deeply at the base of a high forehead. According to local legend, he also had a brilliant mind. He was dressed in a grey wool toque and wool plaid jacket that stopped six inches short of his wrists and threatened to wear away at the elbows. He went about his business with an economy of movement and nothing was seen in the way of extravagant gesture or wasted turns. I sensed his reluctance to stop working. However, when Jay introduced me he looked at me intently, then ceased long enough to peel off one worn work glove and shake my hand. Seeing how busy he was, I felt flattered. I had heard that out of the surrounding chaos Fritz had built his own washing machine, motorbike, and sawmill, to name but a few of his creations. To top it off, much of the population in Iskut Village depended on him to fix their trucks, televisions, chainsaws, snowmobiles, and all-terrain cycles.

The owner of the pickup, squinting up at the same circling swans I had seen minutes before, noted that a lot of people wished they had wings but he thought it would be extremely hard to fly. He then handed Fritz a fifty dollar bill and drove away.

While Jay chattered on about solar power and sawmills, and Fritz largely listened, my eyes toured, then latched onto the house Fritz had built a short distance south. The shape was difficult to define, but it had a remarkable number of angles for its size.

Suddenly emerging from this elaborate design was a small bent twig of a native woman. At possibly four feet ten inches and not more than ninety pounds, she was dressed in rumpled jeans and giant work boots. Her ebony hair, accented by the odd thread of grey, shot past her shoulders. Her face constricted slightly as she spotted me standing beside an abandoned washing machine. With elbows akimbo, pigeon-toed and bent forward, in fact walking as though perpetually ready to fall, she made a beeline for me. All the while she was beaming brightly, caught in her own private rapture.

Evidently, the unwritten rule of not violating others by standing too close had never entered her universe. She stood staring up at me from a distance of no more than five inches. I had heard that Fritz had chosen a mentally challenged woman for a wife, and I knew that this must be Clara. At close range her small brown face showed the seams of forty-odd years of hard living. Her eyes, caged in by poker-straight lashes, glittered like black Alaska diamond.

Stricken by self-consciousness, and unaware of how much she was capable of understanding, I babbled out a few pleasantries, "Hi... How are you...Nice day, isn't it?"

In horror I watched the struggle that ensued. Clara had a flat nose, wide cheeks, and a mouth like an abandoned mine shaft. When it opened, it was like a cavern already in a state of collapse with no visible teeth to support the idiotic grin. Her words were delivered with a colossal effort. Her very voice was like a canyon echo through sunken lips. They laboured fiercely before giving birth to what at first were absolutely unintelligible utterances.

Squirming inside my skin, I shot an accusing glance over in Jay's direction. Quickly I summed up the marvellous time he was having talking to Fritz. How could he abandon me in this predicament? Without so much as an introduction I was left with an enthusiastic, yet mentally challenged woman who stood too close for comfort. How could I make conversation when I didn't understand a single word that struggled from her damp lips?

Impulsively glancing down, I realized Clara and I had the same oblong plastic buttons on our coats. In fact they were the same maroon colour and were both designed with underlying vests. We were, in truth, wearing identical coats. But there was one difference. Clara had all of her buttons done up while all of mine, apart from one, were missing. Nervously I did and undid the sole survivor.

Clara looked puzzled, then reached down, and with dainty brown hands, undid all of her buttons. Next, with great deliberation, she undid the zipper of her underlying vest. Operation complete, she did it all up again. Was she trying to figure out which one of us had the normal coat? As we communicated in coat language, zipping and un-buttoning, a brisk wind caused Clara's eyes to water. With a shiver I reached into my pockets for the mittens I had grabbed off a shelf before leaving. But my thumbs would go only halfway into the holes. What I had picked up in haste was a pair I had made for Ben. Clara watched me fumble with avid interest. Then, heavy-jawed, she stood astride and listened while I jabbered an explanation about why my mittens were too small. As she stared silently up at me, all of my words rang ridiculous in my own ears. Like quicksilver, her expression changed from a sweet smile to a sad crumpled look and back again. Her face revealed such a panorama of moods that I began to wonder if she was simply a reflection of my own transient expression.

Glancing over toward the men I let a sigh of relief escape when I noticed that Jay had started checking his pockets for the key and angling toward the truck, sure signs he was ready to leave. I felt released from a confusing entanglement. It was born not only of terrible pity, but also my own inability to break loose of the custom of communicating foremost in words.

From the door of the Handels' hut, a small face peeked out. Then another popped out from a hiding place in the woodshed. I had been deeply shy as a child, and a vein of it still ran through me. I fully understood how the compulsion to hide could win out over the risk of meeting strangers. Both children were wraith thin. But each at different moments smiled and said "Hi" from beneath caps of straight dark hair. A rich smell of boiling soup wafted out of the angular house.

As great relief and the swans passed through again, I lifted a hand and said, "Well, good-bye. It was nice to meet you." In response, an anxious garble of sound erupted from Clara's mouth. Although I couldn't be sure, I thought she might have said, "Glad you meet me. See you." As she wrestled the words out, wisps of hair were being blown across her furrowed face like grass on the prairie. One more wave and I turned and hightailed it for the pickup truck.

An hour later, as we sat within the varnished log walls of Tattoga Restaurant and consumed our anniversary dinner, I chewed over in my mind the mystery of it all. Dining out was as rare as the beefsteaks we now ate while watching cowboys wail out their best on a black-and-white television set on the counter. The other half of Jay's attention was focussed on a magazine, while his chewing was made discreet by the presence of his bushy beard. Since the restaurant was shutting down for the season, no fresh baking was available. Dessert was ancient cherry pie and bottom-of-the-barrel ice cream. As I nibbled at it, the question circled my brain again. How had Fritz and Clara ended up together?

As a treat for Natalia and Ben, I bought them each a chocolate bar, and on the drive home through the darkness, Jay commented that buying chocolate supported the destruction of the tropical rain forests and that buying gasoline boosted the profits made by Exxon. I suddenly felt silly for my extravagant spending, as well as my desire to go on such a frivolous outing. Grimly, he parked off the highway and we headed back on foot. A short distance down the trail my flashlight died and I had to navigate the twisted roots and sinkholes with the splashes of light Jay sporadically tossed back to me from the sole functioning flashlight.

I felt content to walk through the darkened woods as the trees bordering the trail and lining the ridges high above the creek pointed out the stars. Meanwhile the mystery dangled in front of my face. Why had Fritz married Clara? Was she the kind of woman he wanted? How could he marry someone he couldn't even talk to? Closer to home I puzzled, what on earth did Clara have to do with me?

# Clara's First Visit to the Valley

I didn't see Clara again until six months later in the spring of 1990. After a long winter, Natalia and I had taken a much needed break from the bush in early May and had spent four days visiting friends in Stewart. Rising early on a Saturday morning, we had thumbed a ride the 120 miles back to the Ningunsaw Valley. As we crawled down the side of the towering transport truck, my daughter and I waved a final thank-you to the driver, hoisted our packs, and trotted down the trail. As always after a trip to town, we were eager to set out on foot for home.

Birch and alder saplings growing among the grass snatched at our packs as we passed. But only a short distance from the road, we were brought to an abrupt halt by the sight of an intruder.

"Whose is that?" Nat asked accusingly, furrowing her brow. A seasoned and reliable-looking brown truck loomed to the left of the trail. On its back was a bulky wooden camper, out of the top of which protruded a tall black stovepipe.

All the way home down the leaf-padded trail we tried to guess who was visiting. Beside the path fiddlehead ferns and tiny violets nudged their way through the black soil and the memory of winter.

Natalia was eager to tell her father and brother about our sighting just north of Meziadin Junction. We had screeched to a halt while a wolverine, with tremendous dignity, took its leisurely time crossing the road.

Inwardly I was chortling. In my backpack was a letter of acceptance from Peter Fossel, the editor of *Country Journal*, for a feature story I had written. The letter hadn't simply accepted. It had praised. I was keen on sharing my success with Jay, as well as the town treats in my pack, including cheese, a large bag of nacho chips, and a bottle of ketchup. Still echoing in my ears was the laughter I had shared with Pat and Janet, two women I always saw while in town. I had met Pat during my first winter in the north, and she and her husband, Brian, and two children faithfully arrived in our valley each June to celebrate Natalia's birthday. Pat, with her cap of dark hair and glittering green eyes, was compassionate and able bodied, and over time we had grown close. She had been with me when I gave birth to my son, and had helped me through the labour Jay had been unable to attend. The heartfelt conversations Pat and I shared in the evening, when the children were in bed, were vital to my health. The fact that they only occurred every three or even six months made them all the more poignant. In my pack also nestled letters from my family. My twin sister, Donna, wrote of the most recent antics of her three sons, while my mother told of her latest getaway trip to Reno.

As Natalia and I climbed the last rise before home I breathed in the forest air. It held the promise of renewal. All the way through the mixed blessing of grass and new nettles, we tried to guess who was visiting. Just before we crested the last hill I flashed on the Handels.

Finally our eyes feasted on the familiar gingerbread house hugging the hill. The yard stretched east from the house for 150 feet, and a ragged clump of birch trees, left at my request, flourished at its edge. At the base of the hill, Natty Creek took a sharp turn from its southerly course and headed west. East across the pond on the opposite side of the yard was a two-hundred-foot-tall, tree-lined ridge. Together our eyes darted toward a group of people standing beside our handmade pond forty feet below. There I caught the brightness of Clara's face as she spotted me.

Natalia and I watched with amazement as the small bent figure swung, as though stiff from the saddle, up the path toward us. Overjoyed to see us, she hobbled along bellowing forth her bliss. Her greasy knotted hair was pulled into a matted ponytail at the back and her high cheekbones shone with inner rapture. Below I could see Fritz and Jay, with Ben beside him, engaged in a lively discussion.

Clara seemed half my size as she lunged passionately toward me. Despite this being only our second meeting, she threw her arms around me and embraced me fiercely. Natalia watched astonished as my ears turned an uncharacteristic red and I weakly hugged her back.

Right behind limped one of her children. I recognized the bareboned frame and uncombed pageboy as belonging to the child who had peeked from the doorway up at Iskut. With an attractive mouth and strong teeth, the youth grinned away at Clara's display of affection. But when the child began to speak, I realized that I understood the words even less than those that struggled out of her mother. Clara came to my rescue. Grabbing at the sleeve of her child's pink nylon jacket, she delivered an introduction, "Dis my girl, Julie ANNE!"

Julie's nose sat close to a somewhat sullen face, but she broke into a smile when Nat and I said "Hello." The poor child, mentally challenged like Clara, was further disadvantaged by a deformed hip, the result of one leg being longer than the other.

Beaming with immense pride, Clara hollered, "Chay pa ackt meee!" I smiled nervously, not knowing what she was talking about. Then shedding my pack, I fled to the pond. The girls were hot on my trail.

Ben dashed over, delighted to see me, and I hugged him tightly while he responded with dimples and a strong squeeze.

I soon learned the source of Clara's euphoria. Jay explained how he had led the Handel family on a three-mile hike around the three-hundred-acre river flat upon which our homestead was located. However, they had been brought to a quick halt at one of my favourite spots to the west. We called it Cottonwood Corner: a curiosity of clay oozing from the leaf-buried hillside, and the powerful presence of a grove of northern black cottonwood trees. Some had circumferences of up to twenty feet. Due to spring runoff, the grove was ankle-deep in water.

Jay was keen on winning the Handels over and luring them to the Ningunsaw Valley. Gallantly, he had hoisted Clara onto his back and carried her across. I could imagine him striding easily over submerged logs and limbs while new leaves spun high above the elephantine trunks. Clara would have clung like a spider, putting all of her trust in her steed.

Taking great pains Clara described her journey around the loop trail, but I didn't catch much of it besides the repeated wail of "Chay pa ackt meee!"

Before long, Jay and Fritz had retreated into the dampness of the wheelhouse. After nine years of using kerosene to pilot us through the long winter darkness, Jay had put together our hydroelectric system two years before. Most of the hard labour was in building the six-foot-tall, 150-foot earth-fill dam. This had all been done with picks and shovels and a heavy handmade wheelbarrow. The resulting excavation had become a pathway to the pond. To house the wheel, transmission, and generator, Jay had assembled this ten-foot-square spruce log cabin. Shyly I followed them in.

Once again I was struck by Fritz's appearance. He was tall and somewhat loosely connected in his joints, with black near forbidding eyes and a high forehead traversed by pointed eyebrows. At the nape of his neck sat a small ponytail. Beneath the more obvious humility he had a great deal of dignity. As my husband showed his new friend the system, I quietly watched.

Jay had spent the snowbound months of the winter of 1987 crafting the six-foot-diameter plywood wheel. What had originally been a robin's egg blue had become grease smeared and dull, but it provided us with enough electricity to light our bush home. A square underground chute directed the water from the pond to the wheel, which was mounted on a stainless steel shaft and operated a twelve-volt generator by belts, chains, and pulleys. A heavy electrical cable brought the power 150 feet to the storage batteries inside our house. Only because the wheel was shut down for the moment was conversation possible.

"My story was accepted," I chirped, unable to keep the news to myself any longer.

"Good for you," Jay said. But my success was granted only brief acknowledgement by both men, and then their conversation went the way of belts, batteries, pulleys, and turbines.

I retreated and climbed the hill to the kitchen. As Natalia, Ben, Clara, and Julie clambered after me, I felt a growth of discomfort starting in my neck and fanning out from there. In a life in which I already felt such a great burden of responsibility, I sensed the arrival of a situation that could very well add to the weight of my load. I was acutely aware of Jay's ambition to have Fritz for a neighbour, and I knew this visit was tailor-made to convince him to move his family to our valley. And I could fully appreciate that his would be a positive presence. But I couldn't help wondering what was in it for me. While Fritz and Jay developed a rewarding friendship, I would be in the company of Clara. Granted, I felt great pity for her, but could that be the foundation of a friendship? What I really resented was the fact that these plans were proceeding without consideration of my feelings. Jay seldom spoke of loneliness. I was the one who craved companionship. Truly it would be a bitter irony to have spent more than a decade dreaming about the ideal female neighbour, someone with whom I could right now celebrate the acceptance of my story, and then be cast together with Clara. Not only was she illiterate. She could scarcely even speak.

Clara was right on my heels as I twisted the heart-shaped burl doorknob and stepped into our roomy log home. As she entered I saw her twinkling eyes take in everything. One step up from the tiny entryway, with its east-facing window and hand-planed shelves holding jars of provisions, was the kitchen, the centre of which was the wood cookstove. Pine cupboards lined both the east and west walls. The stovepipe ran up through an open space between a sleeping loft and a landing, which served as the children's library. Double doors with glass made from wrecked automobiles led out onto a ten-by-four-foot sundeck. Until 1985, this twelve-foot-by-sixteen-foot, multilevel entity had been the extent of our living quarters.

It had taken several seasons to build our addition. A good portion of hill had to be moved first, including boulders that had to be levered and sunk into predug graves. Just before Ben was born, the adjoining twenty-one-by-thirty-four-foot expanse, with a full upstairs and attic above, had been completed to the point where Jay could cut a wide entrance through the log wall with his chainsaw.

Clara climbed the step and entered the main living area. After so many years in cramped quarters, my own eyes still feasted on this added space. The most prominent feature was the eight-by-sixteen-foot rock-and-mortar retaining wall, which not only kept the hillside out of our living room but also stored heat from the barrel stove installed at its base. For many months none of us returned from the river without toting at least a few rocks in an old feed sack. Nor will I forget Jay bent double from the weight of the river sand he hauled for mortar mix. He also packed in ninety-pound bags of cement from the highway. The face of the rock wall was intercepted with shale shelves, while warm air tunnels piped heat to higher levels.

Clara responded to the wolf and fox hides hanging in the southwest corner, between expansive small-paned windows, by stumbling over and petting them. Then, catching sight of the great horned owl that stared with glass eyes from a birch branch fastened to the massive log wall, she first shrank, then glowered back. Satisfied she had won the match, she continued her tour, inspecting the laundry tubs against the north wall, and the broom in the corner. From her expression I could tell she was familiar with the basics of household maintenance. She was also tuned into the sighs of a dying fire. Coming to a full stop in front of the Findlay oval cookstove, she gazed at the cast-iron chrome-plated model, with its built-in reservoir and warming oven. Then, heavy-jawed, she lifted the lid and stared into the depths of the firebox. I was putting groceries away and making order of a cluttered sink. Pointing to the wood, which was stored beneath a bench near the stove, Clara sought permission to put a stick in the fire. Once I said, "Sure," she proceeded.

Reaching across the sink, I flung open a window. When I turned, I found Clara standing right behind me, holding her coat high for me to see. Uncertain whether she had truly captured my attention, she took a step closer and virtually shoved the garment in my face. Her mouth opened and closed with deliberation, and at last I caught the words, "Know where I got dis?" A little stunned by the whole display, I shook my head. She leaned even closer and after a dramatic pause shouted, "AT DE DUUMP!"

"At the dump?" I squeaked. Why was I surprised when I shopped there myself?

Whirling around I nervously filled the kettle, chattering on about all of the perfectly good things people throw away these days. Clara nodded gravely and said, "Mm hmm."

Beneath her maroon coat Clara wore western clothes, including a snappy cowboy shirt and well-travelled jeans, the front right pocket of which showed the straining outline of a snuff container. Meanwhile, Natalia and Ben, who had taken Julie on a tour of the upstairs, burst with her out the back door and up the hill to play.

I broke open the first bag of nacho chips to ever enter our valley and offered Clara some. She took to them like geese to grass. Having scooped a heap of them into a bowl, she sat on the bench above the woodbox and dug in. I did my best to conceal my repugnance as, first dousing them with the ketchup I had just unpacked, she then stirred vigorously and downed them with a spoon like cereal and milk.

I soon learned Clara and I had at least one thing in common. We both loved coffee. Once I extended the invitation, she poured herself some from the pot on the stove. Her concept of a full cup was to have the liquid bulging over the brim, then slopping down the sides as she methodically scooped five heaping spoonfuls of sugar from the bowl. Stirring her syrup with a fury, she slapped her spoon on the by now marshy counter when she was done.

"You'd better drink some of that first," I cautioned her as she stood up and proceeded to travel with the cup. Pausing in her tracks, she slurped the brew contentedly, then tipped the mug with both hands and sucked on it until it was gone.

As weary as I was from my trip to town I knew the next task would be cooking dinner for the family as well as our guests. Clara was right behind me as I entered the dampness of the root cellar, where our cache of vegetables glowed like deep sea treasure. Handpicking each red norland potato, I placed them in the bucket I had brought along. Then I paused, uncertain whether to choose carrots, turnip, parsnips, or beets. I could hear Clara breathing behind me. "Do you like turnip, Clara?" I asked. "Mm hmmm," came the reply. Placing a six-pound swede turnip on top of the spuds, I hauled them back into the house. Clara plodded behind.

Soon the air was rich with the smell of simmering vegetables and the canned moose roast heating in the oven. Carefully I crushed garlic, and chopped thyme and celery to add to the bubbling brew.

Meanwhile, Jay and Fritz had entered through the front door, and from the kitchen I could hear them clattering tools in Jay's work area, which occupied the south end of our main living space.

As the last rays of sunlight slanted across the room, I spread the blue-and-white checkered cloth and set seven places around the hand-made dining table at the other end of the room.

"Supper's ready," I called. Fritz and Jay, still in the grip of conversation, pulled their chairs up to the table. I motioned to the remaining seats and soon we were all assembled around the simple dinner. Jay took the lid off the steaming pot of mashed potatoes and began to slap a dollop onto each plate.

"Now is that enough, Clara?" Jay asked. She nodded but offered no protest when he applied yet another serving of moose gravy.

While our German visitors had been present I had come to the conclusion that no one could eat as much as Philipp Pfefferkorn. I now saw that if Philipp had still been with us, he would have met his match in the tiny frame across from me. Clara ate like it was her last meal on this earth. The elevation on her plate was a full four inches higher than the rest of ours. Potatoes were piled sky high, then cemented to the rim with gravy that threatened to escape the plate. Under the table I quietly kicked myself for applying the cloth, knowing all too well the effort involved in hand-washing it later.

With a fist Clara gripped the handle of her spoon and shovelled the food in, filling her cheeks with turnip, moose, and mashed potatoes. In fact, toothlessness worked to her advantage. The void left behind simply provided more storage space as she stuffed and stuffed and stuffed. Her chewing, which was done with an open mouth, was audible right across the broad expanse of the pine table. Suddenly the urge to talk seized her mid-bite. I didn't catch the words at all. What I did catch was the spray of moose gravy that accompanied them. Polite to the point of stupid, I asked, "Pardon?" Without swallowing Clara let fly with another spray of food and verbiage.

"Gross!" Natalia squawked, daring to say what the rest of us only thought. Jay shot her a dirty look.

Where Clara put it all remained an enigma. With a frame as spare as a coat hanger, there seemed little available space for such indulgence.

Her bulging stomach recognized long before her brain that she couldn't pack a week's worth of food into a single meal and Clara finally abandoned her sloppy plate and stumbled to the couch. Releasing a groan, she sank with relief into the goat hides spread there.

"You folks should spend another night in the German cabin," Jay offered. We'd had a late dinner and I had already told Natalia and Ben to get ready for bed.

"Yeah, it'd be tough for Julie to make it through the woods in the dark," Fritz said quietly.

The cabin was nestled in the spruce woods to the west, about five minutes past the far garden. Retreating from the front porch where he had called out a final farewell to the Handel family, Jay stepped back inside, closing the door behind him. It was the first time I had seen him alone all day.

"Fritz is planning on moving down here," he announced, unable to contain his enthusiasm. "I told him they can stay in the guest cabin while he and his boy, Gilbert, set up a tent frame in the meadow above Burl Junction. We hiked through there while you were in town and he likes the spot."

"Well, thanks a lot for asking me!" I fired at him as I yanked the soiled cloth off the table.

"Well, I took you up to meet Clara," Jay said, shrugging defensively. Although it was hardly the time to admit it, I knew that I had made little effort to find neighbours, but my trips out of the valley and opportunities to cultivate new friendships were rare.

What angered me most wasn't his choice of neighbours. It was how little my opinion counted in a decision that would affect me so deeply. Jay continued, "Clara and Julie can stay with us while Fritz is working. They can help you out."

"Help me out? I'll just be babysitting!" I wailed.

"Don't be such a bloody snob!" he shouted.

"A snob?" I challenged. "Just because I'm disgusted watching Clara eat, and it turns me off when she gobs her snuff juice on the grass in the front yard. Does that make me a snob?"

Jay snatched at his beard momentarily. Then he pointed out the feature he thought would attract me most. "You know, I think your getting close to Clara would be a great boost to your spiritual growth."

Indignation rose like mercury up my centre to my throat, threatening to spill forth in a flood of angry words. How would he like to be in the constant company of a mentally challenged person? Already I was responsible for the countless chores that came with a self-sufficient lifestyle. It was difficult not to feel at times that the weight of the work was greater than the appreciation expressed by my family. Each day I cooked, baked, scrubbed, worked in the garden and taught the children, toiling inside as well as outside on duties dictated by weather and seasons. And what about my longing to write?

With her humble smile, Clara had revealed a sweet side and I knew I could accept her in small doses. But as my regular adult female companion? I would have preferred Fritz's company. At least I could have talked to him. The truth was Jay was so delighted with Fritz and all of his accompanying skills that it seemed he may have missed the larger picture. With my throat burning with unexpressed rage, in the sullen light, I scampered up the smooth stairs and flew to the soft folds of my bed.

# Clara Becomes My Neighbour

Clara's move to the Ningunsaw Valley at the end of July 1990 couldn't have come at a more hectic time. Fresh from six weeks at Shuswap Lake, I found myself flung into the middle of harvest season, with visitors, of both the anticipated as well as surprise variety, ready to converge on our clearing.

Despite the stress, Natalia, Ben, and I were all a rich copper hue, seldom seen in our cool northern climate, and the spell in civilization had lifted the children to new heights of worldliness. It had been two years since I had travelled south of Meziadin Junction, and I had set out with some hesitation. But the long luxurious visit with my family turned out to be a wonderful healing balm. We had driven down to the coast with my sister, Donna, her husband, Rick, and their sons Isaac and Tennessee. As we sailed along the freeway, Rick had informed Ben that we were going to be in Vancouver soon. Ben, who had never visited a large city, looked back and forth at the sprawling suburbs and asked with as much maturity as his five-year-old voice could muster, "Which side is it on?" We returned home in August to find Jay grinning proudly from a freshly renovated kitchen. I had done my best to conceal the disappointment I felt when I called our radiophone from Stewart and learned Jay was too busy to meet us at the trailhead. We had luggage to pack down the three-mile trail and, besides, I had thought he would be anxious to see us. True to form, he had used his time alone productively, and as he chattered on about all of the changes and occurrences during our absence, the significance of my own journey diminished to the odd anecdote muttered without conviction. I felt the warm flow of communication fade away again, to be replaced by a renewed wall of isolation, made all the more formidable by the meeting of minds I had experienced while on holiday. Then, escaping from a suddenly stifling house and standing at the edge of the hill, we had gawked at the garden with the same delight adults view kids who have sprouted up during the summer.

Now, on a hot day in August, I knelt beneath an azure sky streaked with mare's tails, my waist-length hair in a braid, my toes burrowing eagerly into the warm earth. I felt my shadow close by as I furiously plucked aromatic mint and chickweed from the double row of onions. Had I been alone I would have been naked. Clara kept her small hawk eyes on me, watching for any movement so she could follow. On one side of us, sixty feet of waist-high potatoes prospered, while on the opposite side, rhubarb with leaves the size of elephant ears stood in a ruddy-stalked row. All of the vine vegetables—peas, cucumbers and tomatoes—swelled expectantly. Pine siskins flitted from pink ruffled poppies to lavish lilies that brushed the oat patch in tones of dusty pink, flaming orange, and sunrise yellow. Beyond the garden, a grassy field crisscrossed with prickly raspberry canes and giant logs felt for and grasped the base of the magnificent forest. Further still soared the jagged peaks of the Coast Mountains.

Wisps of black hair traversed Clara's frown as she held the highest leaf of a plant and asked, "Dis one?"

"Yeah, Clara. That's cow parsnip," I replied. Once given the go-ahead she pulled the pungent-smelling plant out, slowly but with persistence in her small brown fingers.

Reaching the end of the thirty-foot row, I stood up stiffly and brushed the sandy soil off my knees. Like clockwork, Clara jumped up too and swatted at the dirt on the seat of her pants. Next, grabbing my spare shirt from beneath a thorny gooseberry bush and the inevitable bucket, into which I piled zucchini, beans, and greens for lunch, I rushed back up the hill to the house. Clara was hot on my trail.

Back in the kitchen I swung the bucket into the sink while Clara hovered close by watching me with hard dark eyes. When I grabbed a length of toilet paper and blew some garden soil from my nose, she observed me from the distance of a single foot. As I bent over the sink to brush my teeth, she leaned close, her attention glued to the procedure. I felt certain that if I had let her she would, without flinching, watch me defecate. Being a person who needed a large space and, despite my loneliness, a measure of solitude, I felt haunted by her. Finally, with all the patience I could muster I said, "Clara, go sit down."

She backed off without protest and, with her low forehead furrowed and issuing a sigh of resignation, she plunked down on the kitchen bench to continue her stare from there. I found Clara's scrutiny completely unnerving, but over time I gradually came to realize it was her way of becoming familiar with new experiences. She learned by observing. And to her great credit I soon discovered Clara had a sense of fun. One afternoon as I stood at the stove stirring milk pudding she crept up behind me and tapped me on the shoulder. Turning, I saw the small leathery face with the tiny eyes sparkling like a deep sea diver's, and reduced even further in size by the thick lenses of Jay's clumsy safety glasses. Clara was clowning.

Home for the Handels was to be the meadow above Burl Junction. The junction was named after a giant burl growing on a cottonwood tree beside the convergence of the two streams that became Natty Creek. One flowed out of Elbow Lake while the other meandered south from Little Bob Quinn Lake.

The grassy meadow held the odd twist of weathered willow, which expressed its desire to survive in an elaborate display of suckers shooting from the limbs at all angles. Fritz, Jay, and Gilbert had spent the three previous days marking trails and moving the Handels' abundance of belongings from a spot in a recent clear-cut, where they parked their truck, to a site near some springs high up the south-facing hillside. The closest creek was Natty Creek at the base of the hill. Fritz was hoping the spring, which turned into a rivulet during the wet season, would be an adequate water source. The Handels were far from extravagant. In fact I had never met a family who walked as lightly on the earth. Little outside the realm of necessities was ever bought. Toilet paper was old catalogues. And at the dinner table, Fritz reached into his pocket for the same length of nylon thread with which to floss his teeth until it was well past the frayed stage. Crossing his long legs, he would strum his teeth in Clara's direction because he knew she wouldn't mind. The loose wool pants Fritz sewed himself were identical in the front and back, and he turned them around each day to save the knees.

Each morning the Handels trooped down from the guest cabin and joined us for breakfast. They were so quiet when they first came in that, if I was still upstairs, I scarcely knew they were there. Eleven-year-old Gilbert, who was blue-eyed and as lean and alert as a snow-shoe hare, was most reluctant to meet my eye.

After porridge and toast, Fritz would hoist his heavy camouflage pack on his back and head out the door, Gilbert skittering after him. They would spend the day away working on their shelter, while Clara and Julie were left with me. At first they seemed to be perpetually in the way. Adding to my exasperation was the fact that within the next few days I was expecting company and, as always, was in a flap about it, a hereditary condition that had afflicted my mother as well as my grandmother. It was the obligatory tizzy without which the visit wouldn't be a success. The whole house had to be scoured, and I would have to bake for at least four days to have enough to satisfy any sweet tooth five hundred miles from the nearest 7-Eleven. These demands collided with all of the other chores inherent in a homesteading lifestyle, as well as the annual harvest, the largest part of which lay on the near horizon.

As was often the case when there were extra people in our household, life seemed to be one run-on meal. Clara and Julie clung to me like burrs and would have happily spent the day drinking tea.

"Want tea, Clara?" Julie would ask, as though talking to the deaf. Clara would respond with her customary, "Mm hmmm." This was easy to understand, but both females answered many questions with an enigmatical "Hmmp uh," which left Natalia and I scratching our heads wondering whether it meant yes or no.

One afternoon it came to light that Clara, without the aid of Fritz or even a recipe, could make bannock.

"What do you need?" I asked enthusiastically. The ingredients were luckily few because the deliverance of each word initiated a great guessing game.

Slapping the cast-iron pans onto the cookstove, Clara poured a pool of vegetable oil into each. I did my best to ignore the excessive oil, and also the smoking pans. I would be ready with the baking soda in the event of a grease fire. At least she was handling it on her own.

With the sleeves of her plaid shirt pushed above her elbows, and with a strong sense of importance, Clara whipped up the flour and water dough. Then with the fine hands that often sat idle on her lap, she pat-a-caked each piece of bannock and plopped it in the sizzling oil. While the results were not only big and burnt but also heavy and greasy, I was delighted Clara could take over and make lunch. Even though in the past I had been considered a good cook, lately I didn't feel a great deal of confidence. Often I worried that my meals were too big or too small, too rich or too plain, undercooked or overcooked. I didn't know what my family would think about Clara taking over in the kitchen. But on this occasion, Jay complimented Clara lavishly and as a show of appreciation, gulped down an extra lump. Proud as a peacock, she grinned broadly. This experience may have inspired Clara to learn to make yeast bread, which she later did.

Our first anticipated visitors were the result of a feature article I had written for the autumn 1989 issue of *Harrowsmith* magazine. Called simply "Up Natty Creek" and subtitled "Diary of a Wilderness Survival Garden," it had attracted the attention of a CBC film crew from Winnipeg. They asked for and were granted permission to make a documentary film about our garden and lifestyle for *Country Canada*, a long-running and nationally aired program. During moments of insecurity I wondered why I had consented to having our lives invaded by a camera. Deep down I knew why. My aim was to bring national attention to industry's assault upon the fragile northern forests. The vast majority of the Canadian population lived in the south and they maintained an antiquated vision of the north as untouched wilderness stretching to infinity. The sad truth of what was really happening to this virgin vastness had reached a point less than two miles from our solitary homestead. Darrell, a helicopter pilot friend who shared my sentiment, had agreed to fly the film crew over the moonscape clear-cut for a bird's-eye view.

Two months earlier on Natalia's tenth birthday, he had landed his helicopter beside the hay mounds so skilfully that scarcely a straw was lifted. As a gift, Darrell had offered Nat a ride and she chose tenyear-old Waylon, who was out from Stewart with his family, and I to accompany her. The rest waved from the porch as we rose high into the air until house and garden were toy-sized far below. We swung over Elbow Lake and then north above the Bob Quinn fire tower. At first the building was just a tiny white square at the far end of the ridge of alpine meadow, and as we buzzed by the shack looked so desolate I could hardly believe I had spent six months there.

Next we swooped over oblong Devil Lake, set in a forested series of swamps and ridges, then into spectacular More Valley. Jay and I had once had the privilege of camping there on a timbered ledge above a four-thousand-foot drop, in the midst of a band of Rocky Mountain goats.

Nat's face lit up as she began to spot them from the chopper window. Perched here and there on impossible shelves, they were snug in their wool coats. We veered toward towering black peaks too steep to hold the snow that slid to lesser slopes, scattered now with delicate gardens of pink lichen spores. Glaciers gleamed. Unexpectedly enveloped in cloud, we each caught our breath. Then breaking loose, we darted across the Iskut River and east toward the Ningunsaw Valley.

Despite the beauty, I was overwhelmed with sadness as we passed over tiny Desiré Lake where Jay and I had first lived, and where Natalia had been born. One splendid loon floated alone on the smooth water, seemingly unaware that a mere hedge of trees separated it from a massive clear-cut. To have a crew document this devastation would be worth every bit of the invasion of our privacy. Right then and there I had presented the idea to Darrell, and he had agreed to help.

Yet now I was wondering how I was going to prepare for a crew of four when I had two extra people in my hair all day. Granted, Natalia and Ben simply loved having Julie in their midst and they fought for her attention. When Natalia, who could be boisterous and domineering, won over Ben, he would take his revenge on Julie. When this happened, Julie would come directly to me, ignoring her own mother who often as not would be busy boiling her Labrador tea to a stiff pink brew, the pot so full it frequently splashed onto the stove. Clara had a real passion for this plant, which grew locally, and yet seemed completely unaffected by its sedative properties. But when it came to the children she was absolutely sedate and made no move to offer consolation or mediate in any dispute. Instead Clara watched as though from a great distance.

It seemed that if I wasn't dishing out rhubarb sauce, wiping up spilled raspberry juice, or drying spilled tears I was peeling potatoes for the next meal or doing dishes from the last one. I had to admit Clara was willing to lend a hand. Even so I found myself giving her potatoes extra attention before putting them in the pot. The black smears might not have offended everyone, but I had been largely raised by a fastidious grandmother who liked to wear pink and prided herself on never, in her entire life, having donned a pair of trousers. Nanny had worn an apron to protect her pink lace blouses and matching skirts, and wouldn't have considered stepping out into the sun without an elegant brimmed hat and matching gloves.

I had soon discovered that even though her wardrobe was of a more casual kind, Clara also took pride in her dress. She preferred western-style clothing, including fitted cowboy shirts and blue jeans, of which she owned a bumper crop. No matter who outgrew their jeans in Iskut Village, tiny Clara could slip into them.

I will always remember opening the door in high bug season in June to find Clara standing there clutching a huge bundle. In the spirit of generosity, Fritz and his family had packed in at least fifty pairs of second-hand jeans and numerous pairs of shoes for us. Because Clara didn't have a free hand with which to swat the insects, her face was covered with a solid black mass of sucking mosquitoes. With a sympathetic gasp I had reached out and begun to squish them on the little face. How constricted it was with determination!

Later I learned that Clara wore winter clothes in summer and sometimes summer clothes in winter. A blue toque often topped her black hair and glittering eyes. Long before it was fashionable she favoured the layered look. She wore three or four pairs of jeans at once and four shirts simultaneously. With a gleeful expression, she would lift shirt after shirt to show me the one hidden underneath. In spite of her illiteracy, Clara loved shirts with slogans. One said, "Marijuana pickers of Alaska" beneath a large leaf. Another neon-green one proclaimed that "Carpenters have better tools." In any season, Clara never wore less than four pairs of socks pulled carefully one over the other.

In the evening, after the Handels had visited us for the day, Fritz would sit as patient as a saint while Clara, with her nose bumping into her chin in concentration, painstakingly pulled on sock after sock, each a large manoeuvre for the small body. After what seemed like an eternity, she would stick her swaddled feet inside giant boots and follow Fritz out the door.

Clara had other idiosyncrasies that took some getting used to. All too often, in one bulging cheek or other, she would carry a whopping piece of chewing tobacco. Later she would bear the tracks of it at the corners of her mouth or down the length of her chin.

I had never been in the regular company of a snuff chewer and Clara was completely wired to the tarry substance. She kept her container of Copenhagen in the right-hand pocket of her jeans. Earlier in the spring Jay came up with the bright idea of trying snuff juice as a repellent for root maggots in the garden. Clara, who had developed a crush on Jay the minute he packed her over the water at Cottonwood Corner, was obviously flattered that he wanted her spit. She made regular and audible instalments in the glass jar and kept waving it at him, showing off the rising level. Jay was gentle and praised her for her efforts. "Good girl," he crooned.

"Yuck," Natalia complained in undisguised repulsion.

I, for one, was learning to survive various forms of strange experiences in the wake of the Handels' arrival in the Ningunsaw Valley. Shortly after, Clara and I were standing near the stove when she crossed the border of my comfort zone and opened her mouth to show me what it looked like inside. Wincing, I squinted into the dark yawning cavern. What I saw besides gums were her four remaining snuff-stained teeth, two on each side at the bottom.

I could sympathize because I had grieved for the two bottom molars I had lost and I knew all too well the sense of mortality attached to teeth.

It came as a shock when Fritz told me later that Clara had been talked out of her teeth when left alone with an enterprising dentist working for Indian Affairs. I was infuriated by the thought of someone taking advantage of her. Now I felt Clara's quiet need for comment and I uttered, "Not too many teeth left, eh?" But I could scarcely believe my own words as they followed in suit, "It must make it hard to eat." Had I ever seen evidence of this?

"Mm hmm." Clara closed her mouth and assumed a woebegone expression.

Truly, talking to Clara was like talking to someone who spoke a foreign language. I found myself running on at the mouth, making up for the gaps in her mouth, in her brain, in her near non-verbal reality. Other times, talking to Clara was like speaking to a small child. I found myself explaining things over and over again, or saying far more than suited my nature in an attempt to fill up the missing places in our relationship. With my words I also tried to build a wall to protect myself from the staggering irony of having her as my only female friend within reach. She accepted and even seemed to enjoy my foolish chatter, perhaps because for her it equated attention. Or was she simply putting up with me?

To be sure, Clara at times felt frustrated in her attempts to communicate with me. I was so often busy, my mind crowded with thoughts she couldn't understand. And I longed to let my ideas grow wings and soar in the form of written stories, but this was complicated by the guilt of living a pioneering life where every moment spent away from weeding and thinning, chopping and scrubbing felt like an absolute waste of time.

I will never forget the sound of Jay's footsteps on the inside stairs that summer as he climbed to find me one day. I had perched at my desk in the broad light of the working day, beneath the south-facing window. I had only been there a moment jotting thoughts in my journal. In briefly from the garden, slathered with mosquito repellent, with his cap pulled tight, he stood on the steps and asked me what I was doing upstairs that was taking up so much of my time. I ventured to explain, "It will only take a minute..." but he cut me short with, "There's a lot of work to do outside right now." Striding closer, he hovered above me until I tucked my journal away and followed him down to the garden. I spent three hours on my hands and knees sullenly weeding the beets and seething with anger.

Later that afternoon as I did the lunch dishes, Jay waltzed into the kitchen carrying an aromatic bouquet of lavish lilies, which he handed to me. "Oh, thank you," I breathed, my earlier anger forgotten. I thought about what a fine man I had married, a man who had not only raised these exquisite flowers, but who also took time out from a hectic schedule to carry them to the house for me so that I could enjoy them while I cooked, cared for the kids, and did the laundry.

Often, as I worked, I would chat to my twin sister in my mind. Clara had many sisters and had spent her entire life in the midst of her people, and she may have sensed how isolated my life was away from my family and friends. She was fresh from Iskut where, to find companionship, she simply had to cross the road and enter the village. Now, in this strange new culture, she had no access to the mosaic of faces that she had watched grow up and grow old. At times, in our midst, she was happy sitting with the latest issue of *National Geographic* in her lap, staring at the enchanting images. When I had a minute, I would perch beside her and share the awe inspired by the pictures.

Getting to know Clara wasn't the only unique occurrence in our valley in the summer of 1990. The same day that Schwarzy, a feisty rabbit doe, gave birth to a headless offspring, a team of surveyors were winding through the woods in the direction of our home, laying out ribbons. Jay met them on the trail while packing potatoes out to a truck driver who had given him a ride. The two men were visibly amazed to see another human being.

"Potatoes from where?" one asked.

"From home," Jay replied.

"Where's home?"

"Down there in the valley." Jay turned on the bench of tattered birch and, with an earth-stained finger, pointed south toward the base of the distant blue ridge.

The man, who introduced himself from beneath his brimmed hat as Stan, snatched his map from his day pack and consulted it with a fury. As Jay drew close, his eyes instantly latched onto the route traced with authority there.

"What's this for?" he asked darkly.

"This is where the Iskut Road is going," Stan stated.

On May 24, 1990, Premier Bill Vander Zalm had announced the go-ahead for construction of the road that would, for the first time, give access to the pristine and mineral-rich Iskut Valley, and in particular the Eskay Creek property. The valley was located in a region of northwestern British Columbia that, despite its wildness, had been dubbed the Golden Triangle due to its abundance of ore. Furthermore, it would open the virgin valley up to other forms of exploitation, including increased logging, hunting, and development. This was scheduled to happen in a province and on a planet whose lifeblood of biodiversity was daily slipping away, a planet that quite simply couldn't afford it. The estimated cost was $20 million, but the real price could never be measured. Thurber Consultants had done an expensive and supposedly thorough study of the region and had chosen the route.

Jay tried his best to remain calm as he revealed, "Well, the way you've got it laid out, your road is going right through the middle of our house!"

Stan asked for further details. Further details included the fact that it also went right along Natty Creek, which was our water source, and directly across our food source—the garden. Stan and his son

Kevin were two of the surveyors that had been hired to ribbon out the entire length of the Iskut Road on foot. Even so, being a man of conscience, Stan drove Jay to lunch at Bell 11, the nearest truck stop thirty miles south, to hear him out. Over burgers, Jay did his best to convince him that the chosen route would be a terrible one to follow.

Finally returning home, Jay broke the news to me in a voice cracked from too much talking. Apart from pure shock, what struck me most was the appalling fact that a well-funded consulting firm had overlooked the existence of our homestead. How was that possible when ours was the only permanent home for one hundred miles in most directions?

In the meantime, our domestic raspberry crop was being devastated by wasps. There was one wrapped around every luscious berry, and by the time they were done little was left. At least they got drunk on the juice and one flick of a finger sent them to the spruce duff mulch below. If only it was that easy to get rid of the buzzing invasion of industry. I felt our lives being intruded upon on a multitude of levels.

Clara continued to come over each morning and trail after me all day long. I was still trying to clean and bake for the film crew, and more often than not she was in my way. When I needed a spoon she was planted in front of the drawer, or just when I was about to roll out the pie dough she was slopping ultra-sweet tea on the counter.

Granted, Clara did pitch in. This particular morning I had decided to scour the kitchen and Clara found me balanced on the birch chair with its moosehide lacing, straining for the farthest corner of the upper entryway shelf. Grabbing the grimy gallon jars full of dried celery, parsley, poppy seed, zucchini, and other provisions, I passed them to Clara who hovered below like an alert back catcher. She clutched each large jar and swung it onto the counter beside the sink.

Still fuming, my thoughts erupted into comments directed at the only available listener. "Clara, where do they get off even thinking for a minute of putting a road through our house?" My oversized secondhand jeans were hanging on my hips and the presence of patches of homegrown flour on the seat of them, as well as on my nose, didn't add to my credibility as I wailed. "But who's going to care about one little family when they're heading for millions of dollars' worth of gold?"

As I hopped down onto the well-travelled linoleum, I was startled by Clara's expression. She hobbled close to me, her weathered face virtually infused with fire. Her fists were clenched like hammers held away from her sides with fury, while her ebony eyes emitted sparks. Clara's mouth battled to wrap itself around a deep conviction. After a terrible labour accompanied by the shaking of her small fist, she bellowed, "Fight dem!"

"What?" I asked, incredulous. Inwardly I had already resolved to do this, even at the risk of going to jail. But apart from my own children, I had expected little support. "WE FI HIGHT DEM!" Then her voice dropped in volume and softened in tone. Clara left a wide space between each syllable in my name, and the accent landed on the final one as she asked, "Right, Dee ah NAH?"

"That's right, Clara," I said.

# *An Invasion of Visitors*

For two days the rain beat out a steady tattoo while the asparagus ferns drooped and the calendulas glowed like suns among the clumps of celery. We were expecting the surveyors. As I clambered through the raspberry hedge, my arms bearing the abuse of stalks and stinging nettles, a fierce wind flung the black clouds away. The trees shrieked in the assault that sent one, somewhere south in the woods, toppling with an explosive crash. I pulled some weeds from a row of lilies and just as I caught sight of a shrew dashing from a shelter of wheat straw to a cave beneath a cabbage leaf, the men appeared in the yard. With dirty hands, frayed coat, and muscles that muttered to me about middle age, I hustled up the hill.

Inside, Stan and Kevin Brooks were already busy inspecting maps with Jay while Natalia and Ben looked on. Vibrating with controlled indignation, I shook hands with them. They rapidly resumed their discussion, and I raced upstairs, snatching my stack of nationally published articles from beneath my desk. Clara and Julie had gone with Fritz that day, and I wondered what my new friend would have done as a show of support. I wished she were with me.

Strands of hair escaped my braid as I flew downstairs, then came to a halt in front of the short man with the pitted face and piercing blue eyes. My words emerged more timidly than I intended. "I find it strange that Thurber Consultants are unaware of our presence here when there are people across the country who know about us." Stan blushed and shifted one of the pages into reading range. "If I have to I will put my body on the line in order to defend our home," I vowed with trepidation. Their embarrassment intensified. Encouraged, I added, "In all honesty, I would hate to see a road go in at all."

To my astonishment, the men agreed. Indeed it occurred to me that on an individual basis, many would share the sentiment. But each would do his part and go away again. It left me wondering, is that what bureaucracy is all about? No one takes the blame?

Still, the two men seemed sincere in their opinion about the road, and I felt somewhat heartened when they slipped Jay fifty dollars to guide them upstream to seek out other potential routes. As the door closed behind them and I watched them stroll south toward the pond, climb the steep hill, and follow a trail that would take them southeast to the Ningunsaw River, my optimism was replaced with a feeling of distress. What power could my voice possibly have against the roar of greed in the disguise of progress? In the silence that followed for days, I could only imagine the worst.

After three sleepless nights I was jolted by a radiophone call from Stan. What disastrous development would we have to stomach next? On the contrary, the mellifluous voice flowed forth with reassurance. The likeliest access would be at least two miles downstream. I could imagine Stan's eyes twinkling on the other end as he admitted there was one detail left unattended. The government didn't know it yet.

A tidal wave of relief washed over the valley. Once again the rain began to fall, darkening the soil and swelling the hearts of the robins and varied thrushes that sang in celebration. With fresh energy, I switched my focus back to the visit by the film crew.

Shortly before their arrival in early August, Fritz, through steady effort, had completed the shelter for his family. As suddenly as she had arrived Clara was gone, and I knew I wouldn't see the Handel family again until the retreating tracks of the alien camera crew were completely cool.

Even though Darrell had offered to fly in the folks from CBC, I insisted that if they truly wanted a taste of our lifestyle, the least they could do was enter on foot. Admittedly I suffered a twinge of guilt when I saw them stagger onto the front porch, red-faced and panting. Jay had hiked out to meet them and guide them in. However, his presence hadn't prevented executive producer Susan Hoeschen from falling, ripping her pants, and cutting her knee. Nor had he caught the six-foot-five-inch host, Sandy Cushon, when he slipped on a shiny log and fell flat into the stinging nettles. In consolation I served cold creek water and the promise of a lavish lunch.

As usual, I found myself largely in the kitchen, while Jay, like the Pied Piper, led the crew on a tour of his creations. He was so knowledgeable and articulate, they listened spellbound as he explained how he had found this valley, how he had built the place, how he had learned the skills of self-sufficiency, and how he managed to feed his family of four so far from the supermarket. A born entertainer, they were all charmed as he demonstrated one of the many folk toys he had crafted. It was a dancing man with red suit and black boots. He manipulated it by holding onto the stick that protruded from its back. While Jay played his harmonica and tapped his foot, the boots of the wooden man danced on a paddle balanced on his bouncing knee. None of them could believe the array of handmade carvings, including a tripod of entwined snakes balancing a bowl, Rocky Mountain goats with porcupine claws for horns, wolves, bears, and a carved owl whose wings rose when a towel was hung on the hook at its base. From our high ceiling hung a life-sized eagle in progress. Jay truly was the life of the party and I remembered how his magnetic personality had attracted me in the beginning.

A raven cawed lustily and reeled through a remarkably blue sky while Jay led the mesmerized crew through the huge, elaborate garden. It was as if they were each connected by a string and he the master puppeteer. I felt fresh love for my husband well up in me. Sadly it was curdled by the memory of his recent stinging comment about how ashamed he was of me. Was this why he seldom took me anywhere?

It was bizarre to stop beside the yellowing strip of spring red wheat and see Jay, sweating from an unprecedented 90°F, on his hands and knees harvesting the grain with a sickle while the small flock of CBC people filmed him. Cameraman Warren Weldon, who had left most of his equipment behind in the van and suffered hardship packing his camera down the trail, parked his tripod in the quiet harmony of the garden and aimed at Jay. Meanwhile Sandy Cushon, with his easy manner, asked, "Does it ever get to the point where it seems like it's all work?" Susan Hoeschen, trim with red bob and freckles, sat back and listened intently. Behind Warren, the soundman Jean Beaulieu stood somberly in shades, holding the microphone with its foam-encased crosspiece like an avant-garde crucifix.

Before long I learned what "stardom" was all about. With the cold eye of the camera trained on us, the kids and I walked down the hill to the pond, buckets swinging, five consecutive times, trying to make the last trip look like the first.

The next site was the green arrow pea patch where Natalia and Ben refused to co-operate and vanished from the task as soon as the crew did. I, for one, recognized that this wasn't acting. Our winter food was at stake. The peas had to be processed. Paul, a visiting photographer friend, came to my rescue, followed by Jay and Sandy, who filled up the second five-gallon bucket. Everyone gathered on the front porch and helped with the shelling. I canned a full batch of seven quarts and seven pints just before serving a steaming supper of trout cakes, crisp salad, broccoli, and nutty-tasting bread made from our own wheat.

That night the three CBC men retired to the guest cabin while Susan slept downstairs in the main house. I was exhausted, and the last thing I heard before conking out was the hooting of a great grey owl far off in the forest. I awoke to a crack of thunder and a pumpkin-coloured glow through the eastern window. Beyond the deep sea green of the garden, bathed in morning light, South Mountain looked crushed by the weight of coal-black clouds that growled while lightning flared. When I glanced out again, a rainbow shone above South Mountain and shot across the ebony sky to touch down again on the far side of the Iskut Valley. Never had I witnessed a thunderstorm or a rainbow at 7:00 A.M.

Jay and I were interviewed by Sandy right after a breakfast of homegrown wheat cereal and poppyseed cake. A cloud of black flies buzzed as we sat on the front porch overlooking the clearing, forest, and peaks. Dressed in my favourite secondhand jeans and shirt, I did my best to ignore the fact that a half-million people might end up listening to my replies. When Sandy asked me, "Is there anything that you really miss out here?" I answered without hesitation, "I really miss other women. The north is still predominantly a man's world and most of our visitors are male. There is a special bond and friendship that can exist between women and I miss it." As Sandy went on to ask Jay about his beginnings in the bush, Clara's face flickered through my mind. After all, in some sense my dream had come true. I had a female neighbour now. But how could I explain her presence to the nation when I didn't understand it myself?

However, one thing had become clear. Clara had entered my life like a caricature. Her presence gave me double vision. I could see how Jay saw me in relationship to how I at first saw her. Jay was an exceedingly bright man and had an I.Q. at the genius level. From this vantage point he looked at my intelligence in the same way I had started out viewing Clara's. It took great patience to deal with Clara's level, and it seemed to me that Jay felt the same way about relating to me. Yet he was so generous in his show of affection and words of praise for Clara. At times I felt like I was begging for an ounce of affirmation about my accomplishments, work, worth as a human being. But Jay only gave credit where he felt that credit was due.

Each time Sandy directed a question toward me I could feel my husband go rigid beside me, blinking rapidly while I replied.

My only significant statement, and the one that was chosen as the final word in the film, came forth as a plea for the planet. "Our civilization is based on power over nature, and the whole planet is suffering because of this attitude. What we have to realize is that we are part of nature and are completely dependent upon it."

After another day of filming in heat that struck like a hammer, Sandy and Jean were the only ones who didn't plunge into the icy pond. Natalia had a great time ribbing Warren about the roses on his boxer shorts.

In the late afternoon, a far-off rotor beat announced the approach of Darrell, who landed in the most distant garden. As agreed, he flew the crew over the clear-cut, and at his insistence, they took some footage of it. Minutes later, the garden was blasted by hot helicopter breath as they shot low over it, capturing its lush image.

Darrell joined us for dinner, bringing our number to twelve, including Paul's wife and son. From the kitchen wafted the intermingling smells of sweet and sour moose, baked potatoes, peas, coleslaw, cauliflower, fresh bread, and the rhubarb-saskatoon crisp I had baked for dessert. As the evening sun lent an amber hue to the room, Natalia entertained everyone by reading aloud from *Where the Sidewalk Ends* by Shel Silverstein.

On the morning of their departure, Warren came to me and asked for two plastic bags and string. "I do this all the time for blueberry picking," he explained, as he tied the bags over his shoes. I only hoped he wouldn't be trading wet feet for a fancy glissade on one of the countless roots that crisscrossed what was on that final morning a soggy trail. With cheery waves they set out for home in Winnipeg.

Clara's next visit came one day later and coincided with the appearance of Alfred Black, a mysterious author that Jay had met on the highway and, for my sake, invited in. After all, how often did I have the opportunity to talk to another writer?

Alfred climbed unsteadily into the kitchen, almost immediately pointing out that he was manic-depressive and needed lithium pills to "stay balanced." With trembling fingers he took one from a tiny silver and turquoise pillbox and downed it with creek water. Approaching fifty, with sparse grey hair and matching beard, Alfred had blue eyes that shifted from impertinence to desperation. On his lower right arm was a monster tattoo. He parked himself on the bench in the kitchen and talked for the entire day.

Before noon the Handels showed up and, after a brief introduction, Fritz went down to the garden to cut wheat beneath the blazing sun while Jay pulled poppies. Without hesitation, Clara hobbled over and parked herself beside Alfred. Even though he was an expert talker, he didn't listen well and kept calling my new neighbour "Carla." Clara wasn't the least bit offended, and she kept her shiny pebble eyes upon him while he spun his endless yarn. At one point he professed to be the modern Mark Twain while a few moments later he noted that someone else had compared him to Rudyard Kipling. And yes, another critic had claimed that he was a cross between Mark Twain and Louis L'Amour. He and Clara drank countless cups of tea in my kitchen while I dashed from clothesline to stove to sink to garden to pond.

Alfred claimed that his handwriting even changed to match his characters. "Why me?" he sighed. He viewed his talent not only as a gift but also as a terrible burden. Clara, who had been stirring her customary five spoonfuls of sugar into her tea, offered comment in the form of a loud and sympathetic slurp. Alfred ascertained, "There's nothing new under the sun." He was simply repeating what all of the writers in his league, including Shakespeare, had said.

I would have preferred to have believed him, but certain elements
and intonations made me doubt the authenticity of his stories. Not
only had he forgotten to bring any material with him, he also refused
to reveal his pen name. Then there was the nonchalance with which
Alfred described sending his hand-scrawled manuscripts to an unnamed secretary who typed and polished, then passed them to an
eagerly waiting publisher. How strange it was to listen to this author
bestowing his wisdom upon me, the novice scribe, when in reality I
might have been the only one in print while he suffered from delu-
sions of grandeur.

In anticipation of Alfred's visit, I had saved a piece of huckleberry
pie from supper the night before. When Ben burst through the back
door and trotted up licking his lips, Alfred offered him a bite. He
accepted. Clara didn't need an invitation and, grabbing a fork from
the drawer, she was back to claim a share of the last piece.

Methodically she cut a piece off with her fork. Just before her lips
engulfed it, Alfred gave a small shout and, nabbing it off the tines, he
devoured it devilishly.

A ripple of shock passed over Clara's furrowed face. Then, with a
deep sigh, she bent her head and resumed the task of sawing off another piece. Once again, as the forkful veered toward her mouth Alfred grabbed the piece and, with a victory shout, gobbled it himself.
For a fleeting moment the corners of Clara's mouth threatened to meet
the floor. Then with the patience passed down to her from centuries
of waiting for the caribou, she set to work sawing off a piece of the
remaining pie. Once again Alfred got the better of her. In the end,
Clara only claimed a couple of bites. But what I saw in her face was a
willingness to play the game, even if it put her on the losing end.
What I saw in her face was a strong streak of humour.

Alfred finally vanished to the outhouse with one of my articles,
and when Jay stepped through the door, ready to hang the bundles of
poppy pods that swung from a broom handle, I had a chance to ex-

press my doubts about the author he had invited to our home. "I wondered myself," he admitted. The next morning, Jay hiked out to the highway to meet his brother Jacob for their first reunion in sixteen years, and he made sure Alfred, who had snored through the night on our couch, was with him.

As I waved from the kitchen window, I revelled in the brief spell of peace. Clara had gone home with Julie and Fritz the night before, and Natty and Ben were both relaxing with books. Breathing deeply while the kettle whistled on the stove, I watched a white plume rise from a shawl of mist that rested at treeline on South Mountain. It had rained during the night and the sweet air that wafted through the window held a strong hint of autumn. Still, we'd had enough bright blue skies to make good headway with the harvest.

Four hours later Jay and Jacob strode into the yard. Jacob was the only one of Jay's twelve brothers I had never met. He was taller, with a bigger build than Jay. A long brown ponytail, highlighted with blond, extended from the back of a worn blue visor cap. With alert brown eyes above a prominent jaw, he scanned the clearing.

Despite the vow of poverty taken to become a full-time member of the Twin Oaks Community in Virginia, Jacob brought with him wealth in the form of music played on his recorder, art etched skilfully in his sketch pad, and the spirit of his egalitarian community. As chief gardener at Twin Oaks, Jake was keenly interested in our crops. He also spent hours sketching moose with Natalia and offering gentle suggestions for improvement.

When the Handels arrived for a roast rabbit dinner on Sunday afternoon, Jacob put on a puppet show about two frogs and a wizard using puppets he had made from his own socks on the bus trip up from Vancouver. We all loved this rare treat of live theatre.

A little later, Jacob and I went down the hill to the garden to gather vegetables for supper. We had left Clara in the kitchen, but she soon caught wind of our location and clambered down the slope after us. A red squirrel chattered sassily at us from a stately spruce as we bent and harvested sweet cabbage and carrots. As I cut some choice heads of broccoli I instinctively avoided the plant bound with a bright yellow ribbon. Jay had been saving this carefully chosen specimen for seed, and anyone tampering with it would ignite his fury.

At the last minute I remembered I needed parsley and basil and, armed with my pocket knife, sped to the nearby herb patch leaving Jacob gathering pansies for the table. Looking a trifle downcast, Clara had remained a small distance away near the raspberry patch. I heard Jacob ask her in a kind tone, "Would you like to pick some flowers?"

When next I glanced up it was to take in twig-thin Clara with her worried face earnestly holding a huge bouquet of canary-coloured broccoli blossoms, the neon ribbon still fluttering at the base. Dropping my knife, I screamed. Clara was anchored to the earth by her huge boots and steadfast stare. She continued to clutch the brilliant bouquet, gazing at my hysterical display. Jacob grabbed the bunch of bright blossoms and plunged them into the base of a hefty hedge of elderberry and cow parsnips. Clara looked completely baffled.

For days I expected Jay to demand to know about the disappearance of the plant saved for seed. Mysteriously he never mentioned it.

A few weeks later the invasion of visitors had ended. Jacob, who claimed he was taking a bit of the Ningunsaw Valley back in the form of dirt under his fingernails, had flown to Virginia, and summer had faded on the vine.

But this was not a cause for sadness because late fall was a more relaxed time in the valley. The harvest was in and we could enjoy our surroundings. So on a crisp sunny day in October I invited Clara on a ramble. Grinning brightly, she nodded in response. I was certain she wouldn't be cold since she proudly showed me that she was wearing no less than five pairs of socks. Before departure I asked Fritz what his wife did when it was really cold. He looked thoughtful, then replied, "Well, I once counted ten pairs of socks on her at once."

Together Clara and I made our way downstream near the Ningunsaw River. High above the birch, poplar and cottonwood quivered with gold. I stopped to wait for Clara and popped a high-bush cranberry into my mouth, tasted the tart burst of flavour, then spat out the seed. I soon discovered that if I stopped, Clara stopped too, so that we were always single file and four feet apart.

Abruptly the trail I intended to follow ended, blocked by a tangle of alder. Stepping down the bank and onto the river flat, we continued our way downstream and I came to know how much Clara loved to talk. At first the words simply refused to emerge, the eyes saying so much more than the lips could manoeuvre to express. Her mouth twisted first this way, then that, then stopped to suck on itself. Her jaw opened, then closed, and with supreme concentration out came the words. When at last they emerged, like solid primitive blocks, into the light of day, I had to turn them over and over again, searching out the clues, for the point of entry into her mental world. To be sure, at times, Clara talked like she was in no way, shape, or form linked to the here and now. How it had been when Gilbert Dan was a baby. What her sister Bertha was doing up at Iskut. About the accident another sister had been in fifteen years earlier. It was as though all of her life was vivid and present to her at all times, and while she trawled in the present she would hook onto an idea that was only connected to the here and now by some obscure association in her own mind. Being a verbal person I couldn't simply let it all slide by. If Clara felt a need to talk, then I felt a reciprocal need to understand her words. For me it was exhausting; I could only imagine how frustrating it must have been for Clara.

Clara also spoke at varying volumes, from a soft shy greeting to a great booming baritone when she felt she was being ignored, or when she had to compete with other voices. Her words were not only clipped but also merged in unusual ways. Inevitably she delivered her sentences with a punch on the final syllable, which was also higher in tone.

Shocked silence was her only response when I suddenly spotted the deep insignias of grizzly tracks in the wet black sand.

"Look," I said, pointing them out. Her eyes grew wide and her sunken mouth slipped right out of sight down a vortex of dread. It was evident to me that the tracks had been there for several days and there was no immediate danger.

"Come on," I urged, and with a bit of reluctance she followed. The smell of cranberry permeated the afternoon air and I felt a stir of excitement as I remembered how on my last trip to town I had learned that my article, which *Country Journal* had chosen to use for their cover story, had attracted the interest of two book publishers. Sadly there was no sense in trying to share this with Clara. Even though I had come to realize that she understood more than I originally thought, when it came to the intricacies of the publishing world I may as well have been speaking of life on Mars.

The pulse of the forest didn't allow daydreaming for too long. Promptly my attention was snagged by the flight of a snowshoe hare, only a stone's throw away. In transition between its summer and winter coat, its back was still brown while its belly and legs shone white. Clara halted and stared hard after it. The whole while the voice of the forest was swallowed by the ceaseless roar of the river.

Unusually low water was exposing a wealth of gravel bars, and snug in my gumboots I gingerly stepped into a shallow channel and began to wade toward one. Stoically Clara followed.

A moment later, with a cry she stumbled, then caught herself from falling headlong into the stream. Even so, the icy water swirled into her huge boots. Sloshing her way onto dry ground, her words were delivered with colossal effort, "Waa wwaa damn wa TER in dem BOOTS!"

I cringed at the thought of wet feet in October. "Empty them out," I advised her softly. With sympathy I watched while she jerkily poured the water out. I was itching to reach the south end of the river flat before the demands of a dinner that was yet to be made sent my feet flying homeward. I knew this was Clara's special day and that she waited all week for Sunday. But what about me? When did I get a day off? Everyone else seemed to have the luxury of doing what they wanted on Sunday. It was my responsibility to feed more mouths than ever, and if I didn't head back soon and get started I would hear about it later. With my patience wearing thin at the elbows, and with a growing certainty that I wouldn't make it home until Christmas, I waited while the small hands methodically wrung out all ten coarse wool socks. Next, with the corners of her mouth almost meeting the sand upon which she now sat, she pulled them all back on.

Finally we stepped onto the solitary expanse of silky black sand flanked by racing green water. I gasped. On the western horizon across the Iskut River stood staggering Coast Mountain peaks adorned by a robe of bright new snow. Sights such as this had created within me a remarkably strong bond with the north despite the hardships inherent in the lifestyle and a difficult marriage.

"Look at the mountains, Clara. Aren't they beautiful? They're like queens with new silver gowns!"

I heard her assent of "Aa ha." This was followed by "Pttuuu. Splat." As a final statement on the splendour before us, Clara had released a long coffee-coloured jet of snuff juice onto the round grey rocks.

## The Crossing of Paths

The next time Clara came to visit I was making mock pumpkin pie from Swede turnips, while the tea kettle whistled and rocked on the wood cookstove. The afternoon sun coaxed rainbows from the prism that hung in my kitchen window and danced them off across the handmade pine cupboards. As I fluted the edge of the pastry with three fingers, I caught Clara's approach out of the corner of my eye. She wore the habitual blue toque with the white snowflakes high on her head so that her ears were exposed. Her blue nylon ski jacket, with its pink band around the breast and pink collar, was zipped to the tiptop. On her back rode her worn nylon day pack, while in her thin arms she clutched what looked to be a huge book. Immediately I read in her expression the importance of her mission.

Clara beamed as she stomped her way into the kitchen and delivered her customary greeting of, "Hi, Dee ah NAH!"

"Hi, Clara. How are you?" I smiled back as I popped the pies into the oven. Her response of "Good!" was delivered with absolute brightness.

"Where's Fritz?" I asked. In all the months she had lived in the valley, I had only known Clara to walk the trail once on her own.

When she had showed up she had been softer spoken, shyer, and extra polite. One foot had remained outside the door, ready to scurry home again, and her stay was ever so brief.

"Fitz wit CHAY!" she explained, motioning toward the wheelhouse.

"Aah," I nodded. I had missed his passing, and his presence in the vicinity explained Clara's confidence. Now it was time for show and tell.

"Watcha got there?" I asked as Clara slapped what turned out to be a giant photo album onto the table.

"Pit chers," Clara said. But as she frowned intently and rummaged through her pack, I knew she hadn't yet revealed the item she wished most to share. Sensing the simmer of suspense, Natalia shot over from her desk, where she had been absorbed in a language arts paper. Ben was busy playing with the wooden barn and animals Jay had made him.

Out of the faded orange folds Clara gleefully produced a plastic bag containing a pink-gummed and ghoulish grin.

"Are those your dentures?" I squeaked incredulously. With her eyebrows straining for the ceiling, Clara nodded fiercely, then sat down and proceeded to model them. First she fiddled the lower plate into place. Then the upper plate. With the lower one fastened around her four remaining teeth, she showed us her trick of lifting up the middle section with her tongue and waggling it. Natalia and I laughed riotously over this antic, which was performed with an utterly deadpan expression. Then we sobered as Clara positioned both plates with great care. Initially her appearance was immensely improved. The dentures restored the fullness to her mouth and jaw. But as the moments wore on and she sat stiff and mute as a mummy with her unwavering wooden smile, Clara began to look more and more like a weird caricature of herself. "Clara, can't you talk with those in?" I asked.

"Huh uh," she replied in her usual ambiguous manner, and I knew for certain that she simply couldn't sport the dentures and utter words at the same time. Nor could she eat with them.

Soon the air was permeated with the spicy smell of mock pumpkin pie, and by the time it was ready to eat, Clara had spit out her false teeth and sealed them back in the plastic bag. Before long she was contentedly gumming her way through a second slab. It was the first and last time I ever laid eyes on her dentures.

After pie, out came the photo album, and as Clara slouched on the sealskin-topped stool, she methodically turned the well-thumbed pages. Now and then an index finger would point to a figure and she would utter, "Dere's Julie ANNE" or "Dere's Gil bert DAN!" But for the most part there was little in the way of commentary to guide us on our journey through her past. In one photo, a younger Fritz, with a fuller head of hair, held the two children outside the underground home he had built for them early in their marriage. And yes, there were photos of a younger and prettier Clara, smiling with a strong set of teeth, her face magically free of the network of wrinkles I had come to know. It was like viewing a wind-tossed lake when at last it has calmed.

As I gazed at Clara's placid and youthful face, which also held the stoicism of her ancestors, I remembered my own fading beauty, a truth confronted each time I opened the pages of my own album and saw myself twenty years younger. To be sure we were in this together. As women in a youth-obsessed society, where worth is thought to decrease as the years climb, we had to graciously let go of gifts once taken for granted. I sensed that Clara was far less attached to her looks, and these photos, rather than conjuring up regret, spoke to her in a way that language never could. Each opened up a rich cavern of treasured memories.

Even though most of Clara's past remained a mystery, I learned bits from Fritz and much from reading *Spatsizi*, a book by a guide and outfitter named Tommy Walker. Between the two sources I was able to piece together Clara's story, which helped me understand my friend a bit better.

Clara, who had turned forty-four by 1990, was born in the far-off mountains of northwestern British Columbia, in a tiny native settlement called Caribou Hide. Out of a family of sixteen, she was the last to be born in the bush.

In 1948, Tommy Walker and his wife, Marion, were on an odyssey by horseback that had taken them nine hundred miles north from Bella Coola. When they rode into the Caribou Hide Indian village at Metsantan, Clara was two years old. Surrounded by more than fifteen thousand square miles of wilderness, the natives' isolation from civilization was absolute and their native culture was still intact. The nearest supply post was eighty foot miles away at Fort Ware in the Rocky Mountain Trench.

At the time of their arrival, Chief Alex Jack was very worried about his tribe. According to Walker, Clara's people didn't like to hunt more than a day's walk from the village, and intensive harvesting within a small radius had reduced the animal population. Adding to their hunger pangs was the presence of an overfished lake. Already the Indian agent in Telegraph Creek was putting pressure on the Caribou Hide people to move closer to town. They didn't want to go. Nor did the chief see a move to Telegraph Creek as much of an alternative since the Tahltan tribe was far from friendly toward them.

As Walker rode west to the Stikine, the little group waved them out of sight. The guide speculated that this could be the last living example in British Columbia of a band struggling to maintain its traditional way of life, undamaged by white culture. Yet even though they were virtually part of the northern ecology, their hunger would soon lead them through a series of compromises that would effectively destroy the spirit of their ancient ways.

Thousand of years earlier, Clara's ancestors had walked with the wild sheep and goats across the land bridge from Asia. "Caribou Hide" was a local name for the natives who formerly lived at Metsantan. They belonged to the Dene linguistic group and were Sekani in origin.

Clara's people had originally been nomadic. Before white men arrived they had been persecuted by hostile neighbours in the east. Fleeing, they had sought safety in the most rugged mountains. Their refuge in the northern region of the Rockies resulted in the name Sekani, meaning "Dwellers on the Rocks."

With the influx of trading posts and fur buyers, the tribe was lured nearer to the source of trinkets, firearms, and the firewater that would ultimately undermine their way of life. And in order to trade with the roving Sekani, the Hudson's Bay Company established a post on the shore of Bear Lake.

Before World War I, a few families, weary with drinking and scrapping, had struck out in search of a new home. They had trekked 150 miles on foot through the mountains until they discovered a spot in the valley of the Stikine River. In the early 1920s more families joined them and they all moved to a new site at Metsantan Lake. Other natives referred to them as Caribou Hide people.

Reluctantly leaving Clara's people to their own fate, the Walkers rode on to Cold Fish Lake, at the headwaters of the Stikine. There they found just what they were looking for. Sprawling away from the lake were three thousand square miles of pristine alplands called the Spatsizi Plateau. The Spatsizi River wandered through the Eaglenest Mountains and eddied at the foot of a peak slashed with crimson. When the mountain goats rolled in the rubble, their hair became tinted by the red sandstone. Hence the name Spatsizi, which means red goat.

At Cold Fish Lake, the Walkers quickly established a base camp for their hunting expeditions, then left for southern B.C. When they returned to Spatsizi the following spring, and the floatplane touched down on the frigid northern waters, they were amazed to find thirty-five Caribou Hide people there to greet them. As Alex Jack explained, they had no food and couldn't survive any longer at Metsantan. Over the winter the natives had been left in charge of the Walkers' horses, and taking the animals over to Cold Fish Lake had turned into a tribal exodus. Clara's hungry people had set up camp on a hill above the lake. The Walkers had left staple food items in a cache. It stood as testimony to the natives' honour that, despite their famine, they hadn't touched it.

Perhaps Alex Jack, responding to a rumour that Walker was a millionaire, was hoping he could employ the whole lot of them. The compassionate outfitter hired as many as he could, but it wasn't too long before the Indian agent flew out from Telegraph Creek to deliver his edict. The official declared that the migrants would have to move closer to his office. Quite simply, it was far too costly to care for them when they were so far from a settlement. And because there was no money for charters they would have to walk. Clara's people faced no alternative but to trek more than 125 miles to the foreboding Tahltan territory, ultimately leaving behind a way of life that had endured for thousands of years.

When the day arrived for much of the tribe's departure, the Walkers watched with a blend of curiosity and sorrow. Both men and women worked at the packing. Tents were collapsed, belongings were bundled into canvas bags, and since dogs were traditionally used by the Sekani as pack animals, they were called to action. Canvas panniers were placed on the backs of the jubilant dogs, and each was secured with a series of intricate twists of a rope. It was necessary to cart along recently born puppies. Some men carried rifles while others toted crosscut saws. Most of them bore the burden of heavy packs on their backs and an uncertain future at the end of the long trail.

In 1955, the Indian Affairs Branch agreed to evacuate the remaining natives. After the exodus, only three Caribou Hide families stayed at Cold Fish Lake. They trapped in the winter and guided for Tommy Walker in the summer. Walker felt an ongoing responsibility not only to help Clara's tribe but also to save the Spatsizi Plateau and area surrounding it by lobbying to make it into a park.

In Telegraph Creek, the Caribou Hide people stood little chance of ever becoming integrated with the Tahltan community. Obliged to live in tents on a narrow bench of land across the Stikine River, there were numerous weeks each year when it was unsafe to cross, intensifying the isolation they already felt.

Later, during the construction of the Stewart-Cassiar Highway, a solution was chanced upon. The Caribou Hide people longed for a permanent home, and when a number of them helped to slash the right-of-way from the Stikine to an old mission at Kluachon Lake, they saw a way out of mere survival on the wrong side of the river at Telegraph Creek.

Late in the summer of 1962 a native named Bell Nole crossed the Stikine and toiled up the hill behind the town to the Roman Catholic mission. There he spoke for the benefit of Clara's people, insisting it would be best if they made the old mission at Kluachon their permanent home. Happily the priests agreed and by early fall the Sekani were once again on the move.

Soon they had set up their tent camp in a grassy clearing in front of the lonely chapel. Unfortunately, this new location was not to be the secure and safe home they had envisioned. The migration had planted them firmly in the path of progress. Wedged on a stingy strip between an increasingly busy and dusty road and a shadow-casting mountain, the natives soon had no privacy at all. It would take decades to regenerate within them a true sense of place. Already they were becoming dependent on a monthly welfare cheque, and white man's bottled spirits were quickly eroding their own.

Clara spent much of her early life in Kluachon, later called Iskut Village, far from Metsantan, Cold Fish Lake, and a fundamental world that extended only as far as their feet would take them.

At the head of the Iskut River nestles Iskut Lake. The outflowing swells into three lakes lining the valley floor—Eddontenajon, Tattoga, and Kinaskan. Marion and Tommy Walker eventually bought property at Tattoga Lake and opened the first store in the area. There they became neighbours to their old friends, the wandering Caribou Hide.

In 1984, a full five years before I met Clara, my own feet had journeyed through the mountains the Caribou Hide people had called home. In fact, as the small Yukon Air floatplane nosed its way deeper into the wilderness, we all gazed silently down into the awe-inspiring green valleys, knowing full well that we had only our feet to take us home again. A heavily overcast sky trailed fog webs halfway down the mountainsides.

In the group were Cliff and Fay Adams, their twelve-year-old son, Collin, and twenty-one-year-old daughter, Laurel, me, and Laurel's black lab, Bandit. The Adamses owned and operated Todagin Mountain Ranch south of Iskut. They had lived there for twenty years and were one of the first white families to settle in the region.

I felt in need of a break from my domestic routine and longed to explore more of the surrounding wilderness. Jay had cheerfully agreed to stay home with four-year-old Natalia. Some of the few local inhabitants simply shook their heads at the fact that I would take a break from the bush by heading for even more distant peaks.

On schedule, the floatplane had picked us up on June 23 at 6:00 A.M. from Eddontenajon Lake. Eddontenajon is a native word meaning "a little boy drowned." As the legend goes, a young boy had once stood there on a flat rock with a stick in his hand. He was doing his best to imitate the crazy call of a loon that lingered close by. His mother scolded him. She warned that if he copied the bird he would vanish into the water. The youth persisted with his antics and suffered the consequence. He slipped into the lake and was drowned. The native people, whose own history is inextricably linked with wildlife, believe it is wrong to mimic animals.

Our destination was Cold Fish Lake, close to Clara's birthplace and the site to which her people had migrated with hopes of being employed by Tommy Walker.

Soon we lost sight of all except steep mountains and creek-laced valleys. After a half hour of flying, Cliff pointed out tiny Bug Lake followed by Black Fox Lake, and at last Cold Fish Lake, gleaming beneath us like an iridescent boot. Our pilot, wise to the ways of northern waters, landed us so gently we scarcely knew when we had touched down. As we descended the steep ladder, Cliff's eyes misted over with memories. Two decades earlier, for eight consecutive years, he had worked as a guide for Walker.

The cluster of eleven cabins, some of which were adorned with weathered caribou horns, was well maintained, and a notice posted by the Parks Department stated that we could stay up to seven days free of charge. This idyllic location, which once reverberated with the chatter and laughter of Clara's people, sat strangely silent. We had this once thriving hunting base all to ourselves.

Winding trails beckoned in all directions, and we eagerly struck out east toward Spatsizi Plateau. Fay had joined Cliff for a summer, and she pointed out their original camping spot, overgrown with minute poplars now, on a graceful bench of land above the former bustle. Twenty years later the stumps they had sat on still remained in a circle.

We followed a trail that succumbed to the forces of spring run-off. Barren Black Fox Mountain loomed close by, and I gazed out over the vast plateau feeling as if I could walk forever. Had I been born within the wild embrace of a wandering tribe, I may have felt the touch of heaven on earth. The spring grass was scattered with bluebells, buttercups, lupines, arnica, strawberry blossoms, and dandelions. At lower elevations the boreal white and black spruce forests ruled, while willow and birch swayed in accompaniment. Higher up, scrub willow and dwarf birch brushed the sky.

We had journeyed here with the full intention of hiking home, or at least the sixty miles that it would take to arrive at the nearest road. The next morning, while a bald eagle perched on a tree beside the rippling lake, Cliff pointed out the beginning of our route back from the wide window of the cookhouse. West across the water a high green valley, called Donahue Pass, fanned out in an alluring way through the tangled wilderness of the Eaglenest Range. Cliff estimated that our trek would take about four days.

Hoisting heavy packs, we set out under high overcast skies. Cliff showed us the more northerly direction that Clara's people would have walked at the end of the season, then led us west to a horse trail down which he had guided hunters twenty years earlier.

From Donahue Pass we could see in the distance the immense undulating Spatsizi Plateau. Wrapped in sun, wind, and sweat, we shivered as the fresh breath of this new height found us. A patchwork of snow stretched out across the moss and lichen. Forget-me-nots spilled their blue upon us from steep mountainsides.

For the entire day, as we trudged on, we revelled in the panoramic view and freedom from shintangle—the scrubby growth that grabbed the legs. High on a peak across the pass we spotted a magnificent ram. Distant snow patches were dotted with sheep and caribou. The trail we walked was riddled with the tracks of deer, caribou, moose, wolf, and grizzly. With senses strung tightly, we waded through buckbrush that towered over our heads, following a set of grizzly tracks Cliff claimed were larger than any he had seen in all his years of guiding. None of us objected to the presence of the rifle slung over his shoulder.

The first day we hiked the full length of Donahue Pass. Finally at 8:00 P.M. we made camp on a fir-covered knoll at the beginning of Eaglenest Pass. The temperature plunged as darkness descended.

Happily, the next morning we awoke to brilliant sunshine and climbed a rise to gaze east toward the Gladys Lake Reserve. A wide alpine valley stretched out invitingly, eventually giving way to blue mountains scattered with islands of snow. Cliff pointed out a natural salt lick frequented by sheep and caribou. As I stood there I could envision the Caribou Hide natives winding their way across the mossy meadow, scanning the shale slopes for beasts of mythical proportions.

After an oatmeal breakfast we packed up and departed from the knoll, soon arriving at our first obstacle. An icy galloping creek dared us to cross. Barefoot, we advanced, stoically ignoring the needles of pain that penetrated our feet and legs.

As my feet walked on through the wilderness, my mind became the ever distant arrangement of blue mountains against a churning sky. The immensity swallowed me, held me in the cave-stomach of the wild unnamed distance. I pondered. How would it have been to sing with blood that had dwelled here for centuries?

In a twinkling we were gazing up at the trees instead of down at them. We wallowed in the pungent smell of cow parsnips, suspended above us like umbrellas. Higher still, silver poplars spun their leaves in the wind. Insects, detecting the fleeting presence of exotic blood, swarmed forth to feast.

Finally at 5:00 P.M. we all sprawled to rest in the sunshine at a former camp in Eaglenest Pass. Eaglenest Creek roared close by. A few relics remained from the days when Cliff and the natives employed by Walker would guide hunters there. Frameworks of weathered poles marked where tents had once stood.

Our rest over, we crossed yet another fast flowing creek. On the far side the timber was much denser. We clambered through it until we found a patch of moss with space enough for two tents as well as a fire. That night, a staccato of rain drummed the tent tops, while on the far side of the river a pack of wolves kept up a steady chorus. One wolf distinguished himself as an accomplished baritone.

Two days later we came to the top of a rise covered with spruce
and elfin poplar and gazed incredulously at the blue mountains on
the far side of an emerald cradle called the Klappan Valley. This was
the location of the railroad grade, a gravel thoroughfare that connected
with the Stewart-Cassiar Highway and would ultimately lead us home.
Our spirits soared at the sight of it.

All too soon the sixty-mile trek would recede like a dream or a
distant snowy peak. But for me it was also an experience I would
always treasure, an arduous journey through a labyrinth of lonely
mountains where time and space took on new meaning. Unwittingly
I had touched the homeland of Clara's people and I emerged with a
fresh definition of strength. And humility. Indeed, after a mere five
days I felt transformed by the experience. I couldn't even begin to
imagine the consciousness of a tribe whose ancestors had flowed
through the mountains of British Columbia for thousands of years.

In his own way, Fritz Handel had been on a journey almost as
displacing as that of the Caribou Hide people. He had been born and
raised in distant Delaware. As a young man he had fought in Vietnam, survived, and returned home. But two weeks before he completed his three-year term with the navy he realized he could no longer
live with the moral implications of what he knew he had been forced
to do. He went absent without leave.

Fritz struck out for Canada and travelled promptly to the New
Hazelton area of northwestern British Columbia. In this mountain-
ous region he struggled to learn to live off the land. Initially his goal
was to turn his back on a civilization that held the power to enslave
him and force him to perform acts against his own conscience. His
aim was to survive in the bush as the Stone Age hunter-gatherer had
done, and to cut all ties with society. And yet Fritz did not wish to be
a hermit and he dreamed of some day finding a native woman who
was adapted to a more primitive life and of having children with her.

At the same time that he toiled to live off the land, he also came to recognize and value much that civilization had created. Fritz described the five years spent near New Hazelton as being every bit as hard for him as the Great Depression had been for people in the 1930s. He emerged from them permanently shaped for frugality.

Then, at the age of twenty-eight, Fritz ventured further north and arrived in tiny Iskut Village. There amongst the Caribou Hide people he first met Clara up to her elbows in a dishpan. Despite her limited intelligence, she was far from a burden on her family and, along with myriad other errands and chores, Clara washed dishes three times a day for nine or more people. Fritz filled with affection and sympathy for the woman and speculated that perhaps he could give her a better life.

Clara's mother, however, was opposed to the marriage. For one thing Fritz was the wrong colour. And she didn't wish to lose the services of her daughter or the ninety dollars a month disability allowance she received on Clara's behalf. Fritz courted Clara for a year before her mother finally gave her consent. After this was granted, one of the first orders of business was to tell Indian Affairs to discontinue the disability allowance. Fritz would take no handouts from the government.

Fritz felt a special kinship with his new bride, who he also perceived had been through hard times. He sensed Clara was too unsophisticated to be anything less than genuine, and likewise, he felt at liberty to simply be himself with her. Perhaps what sealed the bond was when Clara shone on him what was, in those days, a beautiful smile.

# Celebrating with Clara

"Want walk leetle walk, Dee ah NAH?" Fastening glittering eyes upon me, Clara wrestled out what came to be her weekly request. Above all, Clara loved her walks with me, and I with her, especially since Jay seldom joined me. Earlier in the week, as Natalia and I had pulled on hats and mittens preparing to set out for a walk, Jay, prematurely aged from the dust sent up from the shelf he was sanding, had demanded, "Where are you going?"

"Just down the river," I replied.

"How long are you going to be gone?"

"A couple of hours," I had mumbled. As innocent and sensible as his questions appeared, I felt as if he was trying to control me. Yet despite Jay's need to control, he expressed his love through work. Sadly, the products of his labour were not always perceived as forms of love. If he had only, at times, hung up his hoe and strolled off through the forest with us. Instead Jay isolated himself in his work.

On Sunday, which was now set aside for visiting, Clara became my ticket to freedom. I knew she loved the blatant blue cap with the siren yellow "Country Canada," which Jay had received from the film crew.

"Would you like to wear this for our walk?" I asked. Clara nodded fiercely. When she put the cap on, her head nearly vanished inside it. Yet she wore it with enormous and gleeful pride. The royal blue looked striking above her raven hair.

I opened the split log door with Clara close behind me and stepped out into the yard, inhaling deeply. Beneath a bright October sky, South Mountain stood splendid in a silver robe of fresh snow. The wind scoured the ridges and flung plump pillows of white into the hollows and folds. Here in the valley the birch and poplar shivered, releasing a rain of golden leaves. Below us, four fat geese waddled flat-footed across the bridge to the garden, the sound of their passing a sloppy tap dance. While the root cellar and kitchen shelves bulged with food, the tilled expanse now lay empty. I could sense the soil, beneath the gauze of new snow, relieved of so many of its responsibilities, withdrawing into itself in preparation for winter.

Accepting my permanent position as pathfinder, I urged Clara to "Come on." This would have to be a quick jaunt because Natalia and I had planned a celebration for the evening. It was not only Halloween, it was also a few days before Fritz's forty-fifth birthday and I had baked a cake.

As we struck off through the woods to the west, Clara walked the customary four feet behind me, stopping when I stopped, and staring at me until I pointed out my find to her. First it was the flicker of a grosbeak to the upper branches of a balsam tree. A few steps further I stood transfixed by the way the clouds caressed the ridgeline, which glinted through the trees. Next I spun with the cottonwood leaves, in an ecstasy of glacier wind. Evidently Clara found me more entertaining than the source of my rapture. She would often stand as if waiting for my act to begin and, like a built-in sideshow, I somehow felt obliged to provide her with one. Yet every time I turned on the trail and saw her weather-beaten face beaming beneath the blue synthetic brim, I just had to grin.

Getting to know Clara was like a window that gradually opened allowing a wider and wider view. Eventually I tossed away the "mentally challenged" label and simply let Clara be Clara in all of her simplicity and complexity.

"We'd better head home," I urged, and she cheerfully turned as I turned, and together we followed the trail back. Crossing the garden and climbing onto the front porch, I sank onto the blue bench outside one of the large south-facing windows. Clara plopped down beside me with a deep sigh.

Without warning, around the corner appeared the healthy face of Scott, a young welder who was working temporarily at the Bob Quinn Lake Highways camp. Beside him trotted Holmes, his well-behaved boxer who Scott had earlier claimed would "never make a show dog." Taken by surprise, Spooky, our scruffy terrier, scrambled out from under the bench and stood her ground growling. Holmes remained calm.

Scott sat down on the bench on the opposite side of the door brushing black flies from his wavy hair. Clara stumbled over and delivered a gaping grin. I caught the fresh colour flooding the face of our young visitor. At that moment it occurred to me that we feel somehow justified in not embracing the not beautiful. At first glance Clara was ugly, and I had felt myself participate, initially, in the compulsion to reject her on that basis. And even though the impression came and went, I saw too much personality glittering within the rough ore and I was open enough to seek out other facets. But over time I witnessed the snap judgements made by others, particularly men. If Fritz was intending to keep Clara, to never lose her to the arms of another, then he chose her rough-cut look with care. There wasn't a man in the north who would have run away with Clara, and yet Clara had an eye for the men.

On occasion I had heard Julie tease her mom about different men up at Iskut, and Clara would claim she "loved 'im," whoever *im* may

be. She had developed a crush on Jay the day he packed her through
Willow Park, and she hugged him at every opportunity. Within minutes of bursting through the door and stomping her goliath boots on
the linoleum with a mumble about it being "damn cold out," she
would be over at Jay's workbench.

"HI CHAAY!" she would greet him exuberantly, and Jay would
turn from his carving long enough to take in her face and return the
greeting. Conversation seldom passed this point because by then Fritz
had joined Jay and their words flew to a level Clara couldn't com-
prehend. With a trace of dejection, Clara would wander away to find
me. I think that at first I was her second choice. But from the moment
I had given my friend a silver necklace, her dark eyes had glinted
with affection and she had called me "her pal."

Now, patting Holmes gently on the head, Clara twisted her mouth
first this way, then that before she heaved out the words, "Where oo
dit dat og?" Scott's face flushed as he politely replied, "I beg your
pardon?"

Coming to his rescue, I explained, "She wants to know where
you got the dog."

"Oh. Vancouver Island." Inwardly I chortled because for so many
weeks it had been me who couldn't understand Clara, and I had had
to constantly look to Fritz to act as interpreter.

Her eyebrows flying a full two inches higher, Clara asked, "Where
oo come fum?" No response.

"She wants to know where you came from," I prompted.

"Nanaimo," Scott said anxiously. Clara emitted one of her little
crinkly eyed grins, which indicated that she appreciated the response
but it didn't mean a thing to her.

Next Clara asked, "Is dat og boy or girl?" On his boxer form all
parts were clearly exposed. Holmes was indisputably a boy.

What was more expressive than Clara's limited vocabulary was
the variety of voices that emerged from the defeated mouth. At times

her voice was as small and easily missed as the peeping of a baby sparrow. She was easy to ignore. However, that evening before dinner I was stunned to hear Clara shout for the first time.

Jay had volunteered to make supper for our party, and as he tended the rabbit roasted with potatoes, carrots, and parsnips, I secretly iced Fritz's birthday cake in the entryway. Then, with a cigarette dangling from the corner of his mouth, Jay poked the fire between moves in the "four winds" game he played with Scott while Fritz looked on. The two players attempted to defeat each other by dropping a solid line of same-colour beads onto wooden pegs. The set was homemade, and the beads were awkward to fashion by hand. It wasn't long before Fritz had rigged up a bead-making machine, which worked like a charm.

As I emerged from the adjoining entryway and quietly put the icing-smeared knife in the sink, Clara hobbled into the kitchen and mumbled something to Fritz. He continued his conversation with Scott. At the shout of "Fitz!" I jumped. Ignored again, Clara delivered a hefty holler directly from her solar plexus and aimed at her husband.

"FITZ!" This was accompanied by a solid fist against the counter, her face clenching its own darkness.

"What, Clara?" Fritz asked, slightly annoyed. The increased noise level didn't make her any easier to understand, but she was damn well going to be heard. Clara wanted to know how a brother up at Iskut was doing. Fritz assured her that he was fine.

Her shout caused me to reflect upon my own state of suppression. At times in order to vent my fury I would go into the root cellar and yell. When it came to my writing, Jay continued to be a perplexing bundle of contradictions. At one point he had supported me by building me a splendid desk, inlaid with tropical wood samples from a mail-order catalogue. Recently I had been contracted to write a garden journal for *Country Journal* magazine. It was my first invitation to produce a series for a major publication and I was thrilled, yet Jay seemed to prefer me working in the garden. He had demanded to know what he had ever gained from my writing. Income and honour, I could have replied, but instead I remained silent.

I had begun rising as early as 4:30 A.M. to work on my garden journal in the face of Jay's criticism that I not take time from my regular work day. I would creep downstairs in the wee hours before anyone else was awake. Crumpling paper and stacking kindling as quietly as I could in the wood cookstove, I would curl up on the kitchen bench, using the counter as a table, and scribble frantically until 7:00 A.M. At this hour Jay would noisily appear, thereby communicating his disapproval. Promptly, I felt that the most urgent duty to attend to was making breakfast and I slid my notebook out of sight.

And so I had gone to the root cellar, where white fungus glowed like sea coral on the wet upright posts, to yell my head off without being heard. For years I had kept a smouldering hell-pit of stuffed-in feelings composting in my chest. Jay's anger, when it rose, was not to be ignored. I will never forget the white shade of his face, his fists clenched at his sides as he vibrated with fury.

But I had learned to turn to stone, to bury my thoughts, words, and deeds. I did not exist. Finally the tide of passion would pass, leaving behind a near gentle man with an offering. Choose two days of the week to write, or I was thinking we should take a trip to the Queen Charlotte Islands, or some such token. The demon had slipped from sight and onto the stage Prince Charming would dance, carrying a splendid bouquet of giant red and yellow tulips that he had grown himself and picked. Just for me. Deep down I loved him and always hoped that the change was genuine.

In the cool damp sanctuary of the root cellar, thousands of potato eyes had stared at me from the gloom. Standing among the peaceful mounds of carrots and beets, while overhead cabbages dangled by twine from the damp ceiling, I released my fury. I had screamed until my throat burned and I fell into a fit of coughing. Our marriage had become a battlefield. Much of me went underground, my own self-worth and hidden treasures shining as silently as our winter food, hibernating in the deep darkness of my own inner root cellar. Even as I burned with rage I knew how essentially wrong it was that I didn't feel that I could express it to him.

I soon learned that Clara had a substantial streak of spunk and she knew how to shake her fists like little iron mallets and to growl curses. There was no root cellar for her. She knew how to put her foot down, flat and solid at the base of her skinny shin.

After our Halloween celebration dinner I saw that Clara could also employ her feet in another way.

"Let's dance!" Natalia urged. I still loved to dance and missed it, even though the kids and I, now and then, gyrated on our own for the pure fun of it. But would Clara participate, I wondered?

Once the pine table was pulled out of the way and the tape deck was turned up so that Meatloaf was wailing through the silent timber, the four of us converged on the floor. Julie giggled and wiggled while Natalia and Ben leapt and twirled.

Clara danced as though she was riding a horse, with her elbows bent to grip the reins. Sporadically she would let loose with a holler. Mainly she moved her feet, in a small and rhythmic shuffle about the plywood floor. My friend danced like a blend of native and cowboy. Underlying the dance was the ancestral pacing that matched the heartbeat of the earth. But, like the fate of her people, it had been trampled by a stampede of white men on horses riding the range in order to rule it.

The cowboy influence was contained within her posture and her glance, which wandered now and then to the shelf where we kept a bottle of what Clara called boo hooze. The word was firmly ensconced in her vocabulary, and once she had spotted the bottle she brought our attention to it again and again in hopes we would offer her some.

We had learned quickly that one drink was too much for her. First shadows of meanness darkened her face, and I could see she was in the mood for "fightin." This was a pattern likely learned in Iskut Village, and I had avoided eye contact with her lest I become the target. I couldn't imagine Clara attacking her best friend without suffering an amazing amount of remorse once she had sobered up. Her regret would haunt her day and night and issue forth in meek muffled apologies.

As Clara swayed, her hair remained stiff against her shoulders while her snuff container strained to break loose of her pocket. She also danced as though I was the conductor and she a mere instrument, keeping a sharp eye out for whatever movement I was going to initiate next.

Between songs I dashed to the kitchen for a drink of water and as the music resumed I caught Clara's feet taking a little flight of fancy, her engine stoking up for the rhythm track ahead.

Clara danced as though she could move forever in measured beats. I could tell by her smile that she loved it and even if I danced all night she would stick by me. I thought, aha, here is another realm that we can share! While the men retreated to the kitchen and sat stone-faced in front of their four winds game, Clara, the kids, and I kicked up our heels and revelled in the freedom of movement. Our spinning lifted us above the mundanity of chores and crushing isolation. Even as the moose grunted out its mating call and steep-faced hills shed their skin into the river, we dared to dance for the simple sake of joy.

All too soon duty called. I needed to bring in wood. Clara, ever willing to help, followed me to the woodshed. Each gripping one handle of the loaded nylon wood-sling that Fritz had made me, we struggled back to the house.

Inside the festive mood had dwindled. Fritz, who took it upon himself to do the dishes for the whole crew each Sunday, was bending over the dishpan. Earlier he had showed Jay how to rig up a moose-calling instrument with a can and string, and Jay was out on the porch calling moose. Ben, anxious to join him, wailed, "I can't find my coat!"

"Your coat?" I asked ineptly, gazing around the room as if I had no idea what a coat was, let alone where one might be. Clara, who stood at my side, must have found me remote at times, caught up in my own tensions, dreams, and longing. Before I had met my husband I had been seen as the one with her head in the clouds, but Jay had brought my feet to earth with a tremendous thud. I still tended to be scatterbrained on occasion and was often dreaming, dreaming with my eyes wide open.

Conversely Clara was on the scent right away, and even as I irritably tried to make sense of the cluttered corners, Clara came over swinging the lost coat like a pendulum that swayed between her own baffling blend of inability and absolute common sense. I discovered that in her own way she was keenly observant and her literacy lay in her ability to read the cryptic language of carelessly kicked off boots and other mess created by four busy kids who could throw chaos into any kind of order.

"Thanks, Clara," Ben said, and grinning at her he grabbed the garment and shot out the door.

I had savoured the Halloween celebration, especially the dancing, and was learning to genuinely enjoy Clara's company, but by 9:00 P.M. I was exhausted and in need of private time. Most people can, at the very least, retreat to the toilet for a few moments of peace. Unfortunately, Clara always saw my retreat beyond the yard to urinate as the call for an outing. I couldn't often get out the door without her tracking me down, and I still had not really come to terms with that. Clara was intent on following me to the end of the clearing, to the end of my trail, to the end of the earth if need be.

Stepping outside was something I relished, a rare alone time squatting beneath a velvet sky defined by ivory ridges still locked in the last Ice Age. High above, green, red, and yellow stars swirled in an ever expanding universe. Too close beside me, so that I feared my own boot would be within firing range, Clara clattered her heavy buckle and squatted. Our sounds merged with the hiss of the distant spillway.

◐◉◑◐◉◑◐

# Winter Moments Woven with Clara

I n the hut above Burl Junction, Clara conducted her own business at home, sweeping, making bread, and fishing through boxes of tools finding things for Fritz, her face bright with optimism. She made endless cups of ebony tea, and now and then sat with collapsed shoulders and hands in lap, staring off at the mountains. At the Ningunsaw homestead Natalia and I were now in charge. It was December 3 and Jay and Ben had departed for Stewart.

The 6:00 A.M. air hummed with the vibration of millions of snow-flakes that had flickered down the day before and piled in heaps all over the yard and garden. Natalia was still in bed. I sat in the out-house overlooking Natty Creek and the snow-shrouded garden, mulling over a sobering fact I had learned while reading James Lovelock's *Gaia*—the troposphere upon which all species are totally dependent for survival is only seven miles wide! Shivering from the coldness seeping into my bones, I felt acutely aware of the fragility of the narrow rind of life encompassing the planet. I also became aware of someone watching me through the glassless window.

My eyes were drawn to a spot just beyond the garden. There a blond and tawny wolf lay regarding me with cool curiosity. Then he stood up on long sinewy legs and vigorously shook a great seedhead of snow from his hide. I held my breath as he stared back at me a spell longer, moved further toward the stalwart spruce and cottonwood forest, then vanished from sight.

Just the night before Nat and I had caught the glow of his eyes in the spotlight as he trotted across the snowy clover field.

"He'll stalk those seven fat rabbits running loose," Natalia predicted. Sure enough, they began to vanish and the bunnies in captivity may have been the lucky ones.

Left to our own whims, my daughter and I took up to two hours to feed the caged rabbits because we had to visit them all. Two does, Button and Sassafras, peeked at us from behind their nest of hay, anxious to see what was next on the menu. They were on a three-day hay-potato-turnip cycle.

In the garden Natalia and I stopped to flop in the snow, making angels on our way to the last of the three hay mounds standing draped in snow like Halloween ghosts. The woods tingled with the call of a great grey owl, and the frowziness of the haystacks above the solemn white was somehow reassuring.

I climbed into the centre of one hay hive built around four strips of wood, brought together at the top and joined by crosspieces. Inside it was redolent with the aroma of hay blended with wild mint and clover. Tugging at the tightly packed straw we crammed a total of five buckets worth and carted it to the rabbits.

Back at the house Natalia and I rushed regularly to the front door and kicked it in unison, defeating its efforts to freeze solid. Then, while executing shallow knee bends to stay warm, we stared transfixed by the snow billowing up to absorb more and more of our world.

Bears and woodchucks weren't the only local creatures that curled up in their caves for the season. We also spent more time inside and burrowed into our winter projects. I had nearly completed the garden journal and was now cleaning house and knitting Natalia a sweater.

Housework had become a staunch challenge. Earlier in the fall, Jay had acquired a wood lathe and it was now established in the front room. We had to squeeze by to escape out the front door—past the flying chips and sawdust and past Jay, mummified by dust. Sanding sent up a blizzard of dust that coated the shelves, the stove, the rug, the dog. All matter grew mossy with it. The house plants were suffocating. Even upstairs I had to blow on my sweaters to identify them. The kids and I coughed sporadically, and Jay mentioned ordering dust masks and ear plugs from the wood supply catalogue. The noise made me feel like I was inside a giant tooth that was being drilled. Granted, the birch, alder, and willow containers he turned out were marvellous.

But recently Jay seemed at his pickiest, and I felt criticized at every turn. People outside the family sphere mainly saw the easygoing generous man that was also Jay. But within the home he had a rigid sense of how things should be. I felt burdened by uncertainty, and never knew whether I was doing the right thing. And it angered me to hear him say I didn't see the crud in the corners when it was endless sawdust and shavings created by him alone.

"You know, Clara," I fumed to my friend who stood focussed on my face one Sunday before Jay and Ben had gone to Stewart, "He expects me to keep the floors clean, but not only does he lathe wood inside, he also seems to think it's his God-given right to walk across them in his muddy boots any time he feels like it. Am I supposed to stand there armed with a broom?"

Full of moose soup and confidence, Clara proclaimed loudly, "Cha-ay should kean up his MESS!" Her voice rose with conviction as she added, "Cha-ay is LAZY!"

I chuckled. I had long seen Jay as a workaholic, even if it was always done on his own terms. While we sliced onions for drying, Clara continued to chew on the issue and came forth with another novel idea, "Chay should bay us!"

Clara left the kitchen with her elbows swinging and her butt bent like someone who had just climbed off a horse. She swaggered right up to Jay, who had just shut down the lathe, and stuck her nose in his business. "You should kean your mess, Cha-ay!" She must have had the winning ticket in her pocket because Jay didn't so much as bristle at her suggestion. In fact, when it came to Clara, he oozed with patience.

Despite the difficulties in our marriage, four days after their departure I became conscious of Jay and Ben's expected return and a sporadic crack in the woods or the chatter of a squirrel caused me to crane my neck east toward the trail.

By 7:00 P.M. it was inky black outside and the snow had turned to slop. When Natalia and I went out into the icy downpour to check the weather, it was 32°F and there was already an inch of rain in the gauge.

"The dam!" I cried suddenly. I had forgotten to release a board to lower the level. It was essential to allow more water through to prevent the wall of the dam from bursting.

Rain drummed our heads as we dashed down the slippery hill in the blackness. The tiny flashlight cast a weak eye on a grim situation. The water was lifting its burden of ice up to the top of the bank. To add intrigue to the scenario, a trail of warm wolf tracks crossed a corner of the pond—distinct rosettes in the melting ice. The centre spillway, from which we had to haul a board, was buried under two feet of sodden snow. We lay on our bellies and squinted upside down at the arrangement, shouting over the angry roar of water. Fumbling up the hill like the blind, Nat retrieved a shovel while I grabbed a crowbar and gloves. I was so agitated, I forgot the design of the spillway. Levelheaded Nat rapidly explained it to me.

Back at the dam Nat held the flashlight while I shovelled, throwing the leaden chunks over the spillway. Finally we located the two eight-foot boards that had to be yanked out. With much additional shovelling, wrestling, and grunting we finally pried them out of place. Our saturated clothing clung tightly to our skin. Footing above the swirling water was precarious and at one point I came close to falling in.

The last board that had to be removed was submerged in water and, flat on my belly, I made several attempts with the crowbar. Finally I felt a great surge and Nat grabbed the board to keep it from being washed away. The release of water was matched only by our own rush of relief. The dam was safe!

Overnight our world turned drab, slanted by rain that deflated the snow and saddened the trees. The next day there was still no Jay and Ben, and my mind was going wild with worry.

"How long have they been gone?" I demanded of Nat.

Rolling her eyes she calculated. "Let's see—hay, potatoes, turnips, hay, potatoes, turnips. Six days!"

Jay was never late. They had planned to return on December 6 and they were two days late. I was ready to throw the radiophone through the window. It had been out of order for three months. The Bob Quinn channel, which we were on, wasn't a frequently used one, particularly during the winter, and sometimes it could take weeks before a crew would be sent to a mountaintop to fix the faulty transmitter. Knowing that heavy snow followed by hard rain spelled perfect avalanche weather, we kept our ears glued to regular radio, anxious for any news of the northwest. The air waves gave no indication our remote corner of the province even existed.

By the next day, which was Saturday, we were nearly out of our wits with worry, so Natalia and I set out to hike the trail to Fritz and Clara's. Fritz would perhaps have heard some news and Clara would have some consolation to offer.

As she walked along the trail Natalia made fists with her rabbit skin mittens and her honey-blonde hair shone in the mild morning air. Her pace was steadfast even though we punched through a two-foot mantle of snow with each step. The temperature hovered at 32°F and we had left our snowshoes at home, aware that the snow would stick to them like icing. My thoughts were clouded with anxiety over the whereabouts of Jay and Ben. They had now been gone three days longer than expected. My nostrils flared as I breathed in the damp spruce-steeped air.

Pausing and puffing in what we called Joe's Meadow, we took in the luminous poplar trees celebrating the sky. Suddenly a great grey owl swooped between two shadow-trailing spruce, its wide wings capturing the current.

We followed a gradual slope up from the meadow, toiling north-east along the edge of a bench bountiful with silver birch and massive fir. The trail itself, even with the snow cover, was impressive—wide enough for two to walk side by side. Fritz had coaxed it out of the hillside, cutting directly into the bank and levelling it all with a mattock. What was uppermost in his mind was concern for Julie, who had a difficult time walking.

The upper trail was riddled with moose prints, and at each slip of snow from a limb I sensed a moose standing near, as still as a tree, watching us. I could nearly feel its breath, issued with vigour among the crippled lower branches of the spruce.

Two miles later the trail broadened even more and we were approaching the Handels. It had taken a full hour and a half of sweating and panting to come within earshot of Fritz's bandsaw mill.

As we drew closer we saw him in heavy boots, wool coat, toque, and ear protectors, ready to remove the finished boards. He didn't hear Natalia yodel out a greeting. Finally, instinctively, he turned our way. Fritz never looked too surprised or excited to see us. But he showed his appreciation in a number of ways, like packing a twenty-pound bag of oats down because he had heard we were out of them, and welding new handles onto my worn cooking pots.

Only months before he had arrived at my door with most of the family washing machine on his back. In the Handel home they each did their own laundry, and Fritz thought it unfair that in our house the whole load should land on me. The first time I had run the machine, Clara had pulled passionately on the towels and socks I had fed through the wringer. With fingers extended and hands rapidly twirling around each other, like the inner workings of a clock, she had laboriously opened and closed her mouth around a story of how the wringer always tore her underwear.

Fritz moved away from the noise of the mill. "The day that Jay and Ben left for town I heard on the radio there was an avalanche between Meziadin Lake and Stewart."

My dual track thinking simultaneously registered relief to hear a reason and anxiety. What if they were buried in the avalanche?

Clara came out of their two-room dwelling wearing a welcoming grin. The house held a hint of mystery because we seldom went inside. It was simply too small and stifling to stay in for long.

Fritz opened the door and I stepped into air fertile enough to grow potatoes. The first half of the shoebox was Fritz's work area, as well as a spot for his tools, electric drill, canning equipment, and bead-maker. The family had to pack water and full buckets lined the floor.

Fritz was every bit as industrious as Jay and more inventive. We examined the bead-maker. Fritz pointed out the place through which the rough square of wood was fed, and at the opposite end, where the round balanced bead was born. He had plenty of power tools run on energy produced by his solar panels. High on the hillside, among the ancient willows and scent of passing fox and marten, there was sufficient sunlight, especially in summer, when the sky scarcely knew darkness.

There was an extra bounce in Julie's step as she squeezed past us and out the door behind Natalia. Her schoolwork had arrived and she was keen on learning to read and write.

Fritz was a master of small and a set of bunk beds, with a tiny
window above the top one, lined the east wall. Between a table under
a cheerful mountain-filled window and the stove there was barely
enough room to bend and poke a stick of birch into the firebox. Clara
leaned forward from a chair crammed in beside the table. Her smile
suddenly faded, and her face collapsed in a frown.

"Airs Cha-ay?" she demanded.

"I don't know," I replied. "I've been wondering the same thing."
With only a brief hesitation, Clara spouted her own theory, "He take
the booze. Drink boo hooze! Go on party!"

"No. No. No!" I protested. "Jay doesn't do things like that!"

Clara's scepticism soon turned to eagerness as she showed me the
Hudson's Bay blankets Fritz had washed. The heavy wool was hanging from strips of wood near ceiling level above the little stove. Next,
she displayed the picture she had coloured in the book I had given
her recently, on her forty-fourth birthday.

Clara's dozens of pairs of jeans and shirts were all neatly folded
and stacked on shelves and in boxes. With refined hands she flipped
through the pile, like a secretary through a filing cabinet. She knew
the origin of each and every item, and sporadically she tussled the
name of the previous owner into the light of day. In the process she
had learned to look after a whole mass of material. And she did well.
Clara urged me to look at her fifty pairs of carefully folded wool pants.
She stored some of this under her bed. If she had picked up anything
from modern society, it was the tendency to express herself through
her material possessions. Northeast of the house Fritz had built a
large shed for wood, but then he had decided to make more space in
their living quarters by turning it into Clara's closet.

A trip to the Handels was a lesson in humility. We were regarded
by many as the ultimate peasants, and yet here was a family who
made fewer purchases than we did. For dishes, they each had a jumbo
enamel cup and a generous metal bowl, and it was the individual's

responsibility to keep them clean. Fritz, sensitive to Clara's distaste for doing dishes after having done so many in her youth, tried to lighten the burden and she only had to wash the communal pots and utensils.

Clara didn't enjoy housework and she didn't beat around the bush about it. Her dark pebble eyes sparkled with devilish glee as she boldly announced: "HATE DEM FU KING DISHES! You too Dee ah NAH?" I simply shrugged. I had long since adjusted to my own yoke and had forgotten what freedom felt like. Clara made her own choices and knew that she could plunk on a stool and stare out the window all day without being blasted by Fritz. He was too big a man for that. I felt a surge of jealousy, coupled with the memory of Jay's voice going on and on about "Poor Clara." As far as I was concerned, in some ways Clara had it made. She had love, security, and far more freedom, both mentally and physically, than I had. Fritz gave Clara the luxury of choice and never pressured her to do more than she wanted, while I lived with a man who sometimes seemed like a tyrant.

Granted, Clara was often industrious and since moving to the Ningunsaw had learned to make bread. She fashioned one huge brown loaf a day, baking it in the metal oven that sat on top of their woodstove. Clara's loaves were wholewheat and heavy, and she lifted the towel with pride and displayed it. I praised her for it, and her face broke into a sunny smile.

Sometimes when I went to the Handels Clara was more reclusive, especially if I had a stranger with me. She would deliver the sweetest, most humble smile, letting me know that it wasn't an "out there" day for her. I understood because I had days and longer spells when what I needed to do most was to retreat into my own dream cave. To not have to answer to anyone. Clara had a strong sense of place, and even though her quarters were cramped, she was content to stay home for whole weeks between visits.

It was Fritz's intention to build a larger, more permanent place,

which he later did. And ended up with a handsome twelve-by-six-
teen, two-storey structure with handcrafted double-paned windows.
They gazed down a grassy hillside where wild columbine and del-
phinium swayed among the wanderings of moose and black bear.

The most intriguing feature of the new house was a round underground room. Digging the access first, Fritz picked, shovelled, and
hauled away a square tunnel's worth of earth. Crouching one's way
through the entrance it was possible to stand up in the space at the far
end. Fritz installed a set of tracks that ran the length of the tunnel and
on through the house. As he advanced into the hillside, ultimately
digging with a screwdriver because what he met was hardpan, he
loaded the soil into a homemade cart and wheeled it down the pas-
sageway and out the front door.

But that home was in the future. For now they were toughing it
out in the hut.

"Jay should show up tomorrow," Fritz offered as we departed down
the trail. Clara seemed less sanguine.

"Somebody fight 'im!" she said, taking her own hard fist and driving it firmly into her right eye to illustrate her theory.

On the way home Natalia and I sank into water up to our knees
in Joe's Meadow. Reaching our log haven, our spirits deflated as darkness fell again and there was still no Jay and Ben.

The next day was December 10 and a Sunday. The Handels showed
up around noon. Fritz helped me pump up water, then split and
stacked wood while I made potato soup. After lunch I entered a new
round of worrying when Clara looked at me with wide eyes and said:
"May be somebody KILL 'IM!"

Finally after supper, a full four days late, Jay and Ben wandered
into the yard, looking like ghosts in the flashlight as we all tore out to
meet them. With a shout Clara threw her arms around a baffled Jay.
He and Ben were both soaked and Jay's nose bore scratches from being whipped by surprise branches.

"The road was closed for days because of avalanche conditions," Jay said, pulling back from Clara. "And the bridge is washed out at Burl Junction so I had to leave the skidoo and sled behind." I only cared that they had returned safely. I hugged Ben fiercely, then reached toward Jay. We embraced. So often he angered me, but during his absence I had missed him terribly and realized what an important part of my life he was.

On Monday, Jay repaired the bridge and pulled the sled home. He resembled a motorized Santa Claus whizzing down the trail, his sleigh piled high with Christmas parcels from both mothers, a huge chest of lebkuchen from our friends in Berlin, gifts from a fan in Kentucky, and what was this from Peter Fossel at *Country Journal?* With trembling fingers I opened the envelope and found a contract for $2,500 American for the garden journal. And the work was nearly completed! Overjoyed, I showed it to Jay, hoping he would share my happiness. He took the paper, perused it a little sceptically, and said, "That's good."

However, two days later I felt deflated. As Jay fitted plywood around the washtubs on the north wall, he sermonized that with all the time I spent writing I was making mere pennies. And that it wasn't necessary for our survival.

Furiously grinding grain I choked back my rage. For years I had prayed for a writing space that would surely open up with acceptance by editors. Now I realized that the writing path would never be easy.

As the winter solstice approached, the temperature plunged to −18°F and the air stung nose and cheeks like a swarm of bees. While the woods reverberated with the echoes of popping trees, the mountain peaks flew flags of crimson cloud at sunset. Natalia and Ben scarcely noticed the shrinking days, they were so caught up in the Christmas countdown. Over and over again they whizzed wildly down the hill to the pond on the toboggan Jay had brought them from Stewart. Meanwhile I spent hours and hours transforming my resentment into sweet baked goods. The house became permeated with the smell of fresh fruitcake made with our own dried huckleberries, short-cake, sugar cookies, pecan dreams, and at least a hundred ginger-bread men. The kids helped me decorate them, and on a Sunday visit Clara applied a lavish blue to her designated dozen.

My soul sang in quiet celebration of the passing of the solstice, knowing that the sun would soon regain the vigour to rise high above the ring of peaks and flood our valley with light.

Nestled on our remote homestead we could happily escape the crass commercialism of the festive season. But what we couldn't es-cape each time we turned on the small radio was news of a major war brewing in the Persian Gulf. Ben's fawn eyes were larger than ever with concern. "Natty told me that there's weapons across the ocean that can put holes in the earth and make it burst!"

"Yes, there are some powerful weapons," I told him.

What I couldn't explain to him was why, when we were fast ap-proaching 1991, humankind was still looking to war as a solution to problems. History had proved repeatedly that rather than bringing peace, war only led to further war. I had found myself often exasper-ated with Clara for her lack of ability to grasp certain concepts. But even a glimpse of the larger picture served as proof that our entire species was of limited intelligence.

I'll never forget the look on Clara's face when she arrived Christ-mas Day and spotted the electronic keyboard my mother had sent us. Obviously feeling spiffy in her fresh blue-and-white checkered cow-boy shirt, Clara kicked her way up the steps to gain a closer look at the black box with the coloured lights and ebony and ivory keys.

When Jay switched on the "demo" button, she listened intently. Then, at his invitation, she hesitantly began to press the keys. As her confidence grew, Clara employed both hands, moving them in falter-ing unison. Like a weathered little jazz player lured on by the spell of the music, she became completely absorbed in the tune "Five Hundred Miles," which repeated ad infinitum. As long as the demo played on, Clara could fuse her lack of ability to make music with an established tune. The straight lashes, which caged in an often-defiant expression, were lowered, her black eyes riveted to the magic box. Natalia, radiant in the multihued sweater I had finished knitting her, was itching to try it, but I wouldn't rush Clara. After all, this woman who had such a difficult time communicating had just connected with the universal language of music. In fact she began to press Fritz to buy her one. "Boy, when we get lots money we sure gonna get one dese! Huh FITZ?"

Fritz calmly nodded. In the end it became a bargaining tool. Clara went so far as to agree to give up snuff if she could have her own piano.

Later, when the air was laden with the succulent smell of roasting chicken, I offered to put Clara's tangled hair into a French braid. First I spent an hour wrestling the snarls out with a wet comb. She sat ever so patient on the stool while I, with the tail of the comb, picked up small sweeps of hair and incorporated them into the other three strands. From the back Clara had the neck of a young girl. In one hand she held a cluster of barrettes and elastics dutifully, waiting for me to request them. At the beginning of the session she had pinched some snuff, and having sucked every ounce of life out of it she was ready to eject it somewhere. Her left cheek bulged in testimony. While I fastened the orange lace-encircled barrettes we had bought her for Christmas, she strained toward the stove. When I finally declared the do "done," Clara leaped up. Nat, who had been watching, announced, "Look, everyone. Doesn't Clara's hair look nice?"

And it did. It brought out the metallic sheen at the base of each swoop, and the braid conformed to the shape of her head and terminated ten inches down her back. The bright barrettes highlighted her sleek raven hair. But by the time Fritz, Jay, and the other kids had looked up, Clara was at the stove where the potatoes and other vegetables bubbled, and had hoisted the lid. She spewed a tarry stream of snuff juice into the fire, which protested with a blast of steam.

However, when she followed the rest to the frozen pond to skate I noticed that Clara chose not to wear her toque in case it crushed her hair. And from then on, whenever she came to visit, a small cluster of barrettes and elastics rode in her pocket beside her snuff container, on the chance that I might have time to do her hair.

Christmas afternoon was filled with games, laughter, and some sloppy carol singing. Later in remembrance of Christmases past, I spread the red cloth that Mom had used when I was a child. Then Nat, Clara, Julie, and I sneaked upstairs and put on dresses.

Hastily I fastened gold earrings to match my red dress, brushed my hair until it was smooth and shiny, and put on blush, mascara, and a dab of perfume. Proudly the four of us descended the stairs. Clara came last. Jay's face lit up as we approached the table, where he sat, well back, whittling on a pine black bear. In certain lights he could appear remarkably easygoing, drawling on with a cigarette dangling from his mouth, the well-muscled hands bulging, tightening, then slackening as he carved, carved, carved. "Clara, you look really nice," he said. My spirits plunged as he ignored my own efforts to look good. When I mentioned it to him later, his only comment was, "Beauty is as beauty does."

The main course was roasted rooster hatched in our incubator the previous spring, mashed potatoes, giblet gravy, low-bush cranberry sauce, brussels sprouts, and dill pickles, all locally grown. Dessert was carrot pudding. Before digging in, at my suggestion we joined hands briefly, forming a ring of thanks for the gifts of life and health on this lone green planet of the universe.

"Now what would you like, Clara? How about some nice breast meat?" Jay asked, doting on my friend to a point I found ridiculous. I recognized my own jealousy of Clara but that didn't stop me experiencing the destructive emotion.

The festive season sped by and we didn't gather to celebrate New

Year's Eve. Still, on the final evening of December I was lured outside by a garden transformed into a fairyland by a full moon and fresh snow. My boots squeaked out a curious tune as I sped down the hill, then trudged alone across the pristine ivory quilt, revelling in nature's handiwork. Rather than conceal, the snow accentuated the contours of last year's vegetable rows, and every rise and fold was scattered with thousands of lunar jewels.

When I stopped on the bridge, the only sound was the fluid muttering of Natty Creek, which hurried on while minnows of moonlight darted across its surface. Above, the moon seemed snagged in the branches of a spiny alder, its black fingers laden with the crystal fruit of winter. The raspberry canes were bowing to the power of the season that had invaded. Brown lily stalks stood, their spent glory clutching snow.

On this magical evening I was left wishing whimsically that our species could feed exclusively on the natural beauty that still abounded on the planet. For it opened the door to truth and love, and was truly the food of our souls. Without it our souls would wither. Curiously Clara came to mind and I wondered how much she saw. Certainly my view of her had continued to change. And expand. And tangled up with it was the confusion of my marriage. In the beginning, Jay had always maintained that he only criticized me in order to help me. But as time wore on, he did not always seem to have my best interests at heart. I felt a deep need for support in the writing that I wanted and needed to do. After all, I had been a writer when we met. It was a path I had chosen as a child.

And did he have Clara's best interest at heart? He was far too smart to show anything other than kindness to Clara's face. For Fritz's sake he catered to her and, in fact, treated all the Handels royally, regularly hauling vegetables and other gifts to them on the sled behind the snowmobile. Jay's overwhelming need to control did not extend to Clara and he could afford to be kind to her because he obviously viewed her intelligence as inferior to his own. Clara adored him. But I had come to appreciate Clara as a fully rounded person, not as someone to be pitied. During my blacker moments I wondered if Jay should have married a Clara, someone content to follow him around, sweep up his shavings, and never voice an opinion that clashed with his own. Yet of course Clara had more spunk than he recognized.

He made occasional comments about how alike Clara and I were, and yet I couldn't overlook one difference. He seemed to treat her with a little more respect than he treated me. Jay was aware of Fritz's abilities and he was desperate to keep them in the Ningunsaw Valley. In a heated moment, he had told me that the Handel family was more important to him than his own. I believe that deep down he possibly didn't trust that I would stay. At the same time, Jay was dedicated to his home and family. Nearly every waking moment was an ongoing effort to sustain and improve our place.

As I climbed the hill to the sleeping house, the soaring mountains were marbled by light. As though in a display of hope, a pink ring appeared around the moon and a tide of star-flecked cloud swept across the southern sky. The garden breathed deep beneath its bed of snow blossoms.

ᘒᘓᘔᘓᘔᘓ

# *Snowshoeing with Clara*

"HEY!" Clara's shout broke the silence of our webbed walking across a shawl of snow. The endless white wrapped itself around spruce and balsam trunks while high above, evergreen branches wove intimate tapestries against an indigo sky.

Turning on my handmade birch frames laced with moosehide, I watched as Clara hobbled along on one snowshoe, waving the other one at me. The message in the motion was that she had lost her shoe and it was up to me to make it better. The burgundy scarf I had tied around her face to protect her from frostbite had slipped, and her blue toque with the off-white snowflakes rode too high to protect her ears.

For two weeks the temperature had remained below –22°F, and the world had turned to diamond—brilliant but sharp enough to cut. One morning I had listened in amazement as high on the hill in the tooth-cracking cold, a mysterious bird, which I couldn't see to identify, passionately sang its heart out. In the woods, as in life, there was always room for the unexpected, and I was delighted to discover that Clara loved to go snowshoeing with me. Quickly she developed the habit of lugging her snowshoes down with her each Sunday, and my only wish was that she could have put them on by herself. It was like having another kid!

Even though it was now a balmy 14°F, I could feel the frigid metal of her buckles suck the warmth from my body through my fingertips as I toiled to get her foot placed properly on the bearpaw snowshoe. It was nearly as frustrating as manoeuvring floppy boots onto a limp toddler's foot, and what made it worse was the dead certainty that Clara was capable of doing it herself. Understandably, she sought the attention and the contact. This need had been made evident by her habit of coming up behind me and slipping her arms around my waist and affectionately hanging onto me for lingering spells.

Our first destination was Willow Park, where Jay had recently chopped down an ancient willow to acquire special wood for his carving. I felt protective toward the gnarled trees and I wanted to see which one had been sacrificed for his craft.

For a moment walking west through the woods with Clara, I wished I were alone. Her need to talk was conflicting with my own need to commune with nature. And still I simply could not ignore her. Consistently I listened and did my best to understand. "Him always fight me," she said, referring to a woman at Iskut Village and how she, Clara, couldn't fight people because she was too small. Poor Clara, I thought, and aloud told her to, "just ignore her when she's like that." I hoped my advice helped but more often I found that a way to relate to Clara was simply to be with her and restrict verbal communication to three-word sentences.

Perched on a crusty snow bench in the dazzling sunlight beneath a tangle of alder, Clara and I shared a rest and some oatmeal cookies. "Good, eh, Clara?"

She responded in her sweetest, most compliant voice. "Good coo kies Dee ah NAH!"

We were comfortable sitting close together on the frozen bench. Neither of us took chances with the cold. We both knew it could kill.

I sported long johns, knee-high red wool socks, and the thick blue jacket I wore for chores. The front, cuffs, and collar bore stains from hauling wood, hay, and buckets of vegetables for the rabbits. My giant homemade wool mitts were on my hands and on my head was a rhinestone-covered beret. Beside me Clara was snug in her six pairs of socks, four pairs of jeans, conglomeration of shirts, and deluxe hide gloves. The heels of her giant boots were dug into the snow, her hands were parked on her knees, and her face had become lost in thought.

Clara's face bore the torture of forty-four years of living, for life gets to us no matter who we are. She had suffered and the rise and fall of features and lines had written much of it for the world to see. Gone for the moment was the expression of mirth and replacing it was the darkness of the demons of the underworld. All spirits tramped through Clara, using her mercilessly for their playground. Yet she was also blessed with the divine strength to let them in, let them pass through, and be gone, of no lasting damage to her well-being.

Once I had fastened both sets of snowshoes securely, the smell of wet wool drifting up from my mitts, we set out again toward Willow Park with me breaking trail. As we approached the meadow, what sounded like a motorcycle starting up matched the racing of our hearts as a ruffed grouse sailed up from the snow, then perched statue-still in a mottled alder. Just short of the clearing we stopped in our waffle tracks to watch, open-mouthed, as a giant bull moose charged across the far side of the meadow, its muscular bulk rippling while its finely turned feet sent up bright sprays of snow like sea foam.

Clara continued to plod behind me to the centre of the meadow, where we discovered a freshly abandoned moose bed showered with urine. Close by was a willow stump that thankfully did not belong to the tree I cherished most.

My thigh muscles complained as I lifted my legs high to break trail through Cottonwood Corner. On either side of us rose elephantine cottonwoods, with bark as corrugated as a flood plain. One tree, which I gazed at each time, was shaped like a tuning fork, its mighty limbs resonating with the harmony of earth and sky.

Soon we swung south, crossed Natty Creek on a log, and plodded on toward the Ningunsaw River. Clara was getting red in the face, and she asked me twice where we were going. Frequently when I turned I found her flat on her face in the snow, but without a word she would pick herself up and carry on.

As soon as we had broken free of the stifling embrace of the towering woods and were standing on the wide river flat, I felt I had perspective. I could breathe more easily.

On the far side of the river, the base of South Mountain was wrapped in a shawl of mist so that it appeared to be floating. The entire river flat was writhing with wolf tracks, and as we walked on we found much evidence of the activity of a pack.

Trudging east along the frozen expanse, we discovered the place where the group had slept, defecated, peed, and frolicked. Smaller tracks indicated the presence of pups. Some of the scat was so black and runny I thought at first it was patches of sand. It was the kind of bowel movement wolves had after eating fresh moose.

Above the hedge of her scarf, Clara's eyes watered as she scanned the riverscape and mainly my face. I felt like her magnetic north. On an impulse I followed the wolf tracks south across the river with Clara right behind me. Truly, it wasn't everyone that I would have shared this river kingdom with. But, at that moment, I cheerfully did so with Clara, despite the sacrilegious *splat* of snuff that she shot at the purity around us.

I had reached the point of not really caring whether Clara was clever or not. Quite simply she was my pal, my partner in travels through our region, and we were developing a deep sense of kinship. At times she ceased needing my undivided attention and fell full-heartedly into the rhythm of breathing in, listening to, touching, and tasting the wild paradise into which fate had cast us together.

The windblown reach was calm for now, and the solitary voice of a dipper trilled above churning water that spiralled through hollows where the ice had failed to stitch itself together. Instead it gaped with holes. Shuddering, I gawked at the prospect of slipping into one and vanishing forever. Swallowed by the wilderness. My passing recorded for all time by the fluid incantations of the Ningunsaw.

Clara followed me across the river and up the steep far bank. Further on through a thicket of cottonwood and willow saplings we found a patch of moose hair. The next channel we encountered was merely laced with ice, and I didn't want to risk wet shoes or worse. Reluctantly I abandoned following the wolf tracks.

We would see no wolves that day but earlier in the month I had stood spellbound, on our front porch, and listened to what began as a moan and developed into a full-fledged chorus. While stars glowed through the stormy night I had shivered in the embrace of the chilling wolf pack choir. Wolves seemed to like to strike when it was stormy, and while the snow devils whirled down the Ningunsaw, they had made their kill.

I recalled too how Jay, Natalia, and I had found a moose carcass in the same vicinity years earlier. With noses pinched against the putrid stench, we had viewed the half-devoured cow and, alongside, a perfect pink moose foetus with delicate hooves the colour of mozzarella cheese. Close by were four imprints where the satiated wolves had slept. The snow had been smeared with moose hair and blood and the certainty that they would return.

On the way back with Clara I skied the sharp drop to the river by crouching on my snowshoes. Clara tried to imitate me and, once again, fell. Without a word she stood up, regaining her dignity.

As we crossed safely to the north side, I flashed on Clara's journey through the mountains as a child and wondered if this was where she had gained her stoicism. Her trek was a continual source of fascination for me, and facing her I attempted to draw out some details.

"What was it like, Clara?"

Clara stopped on the frozen flat, her heavy mittens forming blunt tools at the sides of her legs, her shoulders suggesting defeat, while the dippers, parked on shelves of ice over the cascading current, out-shone her with their fluency. Held suspended in the breath of the wilderness, Clara's own breath came in short puffs, her eyebrows converging in frustration. Somewhere within her uncharted psyche it was all registered. It had become part of her inner landscape. Her intense gaze told me she remembered. My probing may have brought back the gnaw of hunger, the blisters, and the need to push on through the unforgiving mountains.

Much of her journey was lost to the mists of time. But the first evening I had watched Clara consume a mountain of meat at a single sitting, Fritz had explained that, as a child, her diet had been largely meat and she still had a craving to gorge. She reminded me of the wolves, which, when they had made a substantial kill, would gorge on it until they reached a state that biologist Barry Lopez referred to as meat drunk. Then, nose to tail tip, they would sleep for a couple of days. More than once I had watched Clara stagger away from the table, stuffed to the point of discomfort, looking for a cosy corner to curl up in. As for her childhood, Clara had absolutely nothing to offer on the subject, and I abandoned my efforts to learn about it.

Abruptly, like a dazzling benediction, the sun spun itself out from behind a forbidding mountain and flooded the land with amber light, igniting prismatic gems that travelled the course of the silver robe of snow. Shaking my wool mitts loose, I let them fall to the ground while fibres still clung to my fingers. Impulsively I stretched both arms toward the sun and felt warmth and hope flood my entire being.

Beside me Clara halted, her knees bent slightly, while the sun caught the shelf of a cheekbone and her eyes held the dimness of doubt.

"What you doin', Dee ah NAH?"

I remained leaning toward the fiery ball for a few more minutes before answering her, unwilling to break from my trance. Clara didn't ask again but instead stood stone still, waiting. Finally, I lowered my arms.

"Clara, I'm praying to the sun."

"How come?"

"I'm praising the sun because the sun is, in a sense, God. Without it there would be no life on this planet."

What surprised me wasn't her reaction, which was the deliverance of a deadpan gaze, but the fact that I had said it at all. Normally I kept my belief system and rituals locked away like love letters.

At times, during moments of doubt and frustration, I wondered if Clara understood anything I said. And yet I knew she did because even if some concepts evaded her, she gave me such a profusion of undivided attention, a willingness to listen to my gibberish and be there for me that it had to be the result of some kind of marriage of compassion and understanding.

Then there were the moments when it was just plain fun to be with Clara. I am basically shy and occasionally an intensely introverted person, and Clara, with her simple acceptance, helped to draw me out. No matter what I did, said, or felt, she remained my friend. After being under the scrutiny of an increasingly disapproving husband, this felt like delicious freedom. In her own way Clara showed her support. She knew by then that I was in a marriage with a partner who wielded a number of weapons, perhaps the most potent of which was withholding affection. Little wobbly Clara wanted to protect me from it, and in her tangled tongue she laid it out, moving one open hand up and down to emphasize her point.

"If Cha-ay bodder you. YOU COME STAY BY US!" As she delivered the proclamation, her eyes hardened and her index finger attacked her own chest in a staccato of passion.

As difficult as it was for me to imagine three more people living in the Handel hut, because of course the children and I were a package deal, I deeply appreciated the offer, and the caring behind her words.

Clara was also very tactile and at first I found myself cringing from her touch. Yet as much as I found her advances initially intrusive, I came to appreciate the hug that followed each Sunday dinner. It was somehow healing when this curious woman, without reservation, reached up and put her thin leathery arms around me and held me in the most maternal way.

Clara didn't judge me, had no capacity to judge, and I felt more accepted by her than by most women. In our society so much of our short life span is consumed measuring our achievements and clambering up the ladder to so-called success. Clara was one of the rare ones who was willing to wait and let life unfold its gifts in its own time and way.

I set out once again, west this time toward my favourite mountains on the far side of the Iskut River. Behind me Clara trudged on, another entity of womanspirit moving forever across the frozen river flat, scanning with humility the pristine peaks inflamed with the light of the sunset. Snowshoeing with Clara held the rhythm of wading through clouds, on our way to nowhere, stuck in the mountain-valley of *now* in a profound and endless way. I felt free with Clara wandering the frozen expanse, as linked as any migrating herd, following ancient trails that existed in the memories of rock and wild beings. Over and over again I found my songs, gestures, and thoughts met with cheerful acceptance.

Impulsively I stopped, unbuckled my snowshoes and stuck them in the snow. Facing a plump pillow that covered a swell of sand, I flopped into it face first. Instantly my head created a crystal cave, but I wasn't done. Lying prone, I rolled across the rippling ivory quilt. Glancing back, I caught Clara's twinkle as she viewed my antics.

"Want to try it?" I called. She nodded earnestly and advanced to a point where I could undo her snowshoes for her. Without them we sank without resistance into the mounds, where mouse trails left cryptic messages that vanished into tunnels and snow-shrouded driftwood cut curious figures. Crawling was easier than walking and Clara crept playfully behind me.

"Wa ter, wa ter," I moaned, pretending to be traversing the Sahara Desert on all fours. Behind me, on hands and knees, Clara parroted my words. With total abandonment, I threw my head back and began to wail like a wolf. Clara's hesitant voice merged with mine as we crawled and howled our way across an expanse that was riddled with real wolf tracks, produced by a pack that may have still lingered close by. Perhaps they were crouching in the timber, with heads cocked, listening to us howl our hearts out, but who else would ever know besides Clara, the river, and me?

Regularly my friend reminded me of the little child in residence in each of us, and she released the small one within me. When so much of my life had become serious, she made me want to laugh and play.

But Clara also had the misfortune of learning just how uncommunicative I could be. At times I needed to think my own thoughts, not to be dragged through the impossible maze of a separate psyche. I found myself slipping into this mood as, exasperated, I forced Clara's snowshoes back on her goliath boots. I had skipped lunch that day and the three-mile trudge, plus the antics on the flat, had sapped me of my energy. Weary and irritable, I pushed back toward the woods and home. Clara, who was struggling to keep up, had a sudden urge to chatter, and I tossed away the word webs she was spinning to entangle me. I was happy weaving bright tapestries in my own brain, taking my own blend of thought, experience, and gifts from the unconscious, my own life story, and filling up my day with it. I had been remembering what it had been like to wander through the emerald fields on the Isle of Skye, with the sea far below. I had been such a gypsy then, and now I felt as rooted in this valley as any tree that had thrived here for a century. I wanted time and psychic space to ponder the flying dream I had had recently, where I had soared like a raven above the earth, with a child under each arm. Craving solitude, I rushed ahead down the trail graced with refined spruce and giant cottonwood.

At last, chest heaving, I stopped in my tracks, lifted each amber-laced shoe high, and turned. Beneath the snow, the devil's club still brandished its thorns, while high above, the shadow of a passing raven still hung in the balsam branches. As a squirrel scolding incessantly darted to a higher branch, I stopped and turned to look at Clara.

Walking behind me was a middle-aged native woman with a face exuding delight in the moment. She was happy simply to be moving through the forest with me, her pal, her buddy like no other. At that moment my frustration fell away like rotting April snow and softly I asked her, "How are you doing, Clara?"

Stumbling along with one bear paw ready to escape, she advanced down the path defined by snow hedges. Pulling up close to me she delivered her predictable reply. "Good!" But it was delivered with eyes that took me in with immense and timeless humour.

# Books and Barn Building

C lara was visiting one bright March afternoon and had just taken my wash off the line for me. I appreciated how cheerfully she came into the kitchen, her arms bulging with sweet-smelling laundry. Jay, in his red beret, was on his way through the house. He made a suggestion that was not quite as cheerful. "You could dig four big holes in the snow to mark the corners of the new chicken house. Then we could start moving logs down to the site right away."

"Want to come, Clara?" I asked, turning to my friend. Her black eyebrows flew like swallows as she nodded eagerly in response. She followed me out the back door to the woodshed, where I retrieved a shovel. Then together we trudged east to the location of the new chicken house, her face all seriousness above her plaid collar.

A ripe wind snapped at the tape measure as I marked out a twelve-by-fifteen-foot square on top of the solid crust of snow. Once the corners were established, I heaved the heavy cakes out with the shovel, puffing and grunting. As I dug deeper, knowing there were three more holes to go, Clara simply stood above me on the slowly rising edge. Normally she was more than willing to pitch in, but today she made absolutely no move to help. This irked me because the snow was like lead and I could have used a hand. The presence of a passive audience only added to my burden.

As I grew increasingly crimson-faced and frustrated, my buddy stood staring down at me from an ever higher vantage point, looking dismal and shaking her head.

Finally, as I stood clutching the shovel, it flashed through my mind that this was not the native way. This was pushing the river. Clara had been raised by the simple Sekani philosophy that allowed each day to take care of itself. Any self-respecting Caribou Hide native would have waited for the snow to melt and then started to build.

"You think this is crazy, don't you?"

"Mm hmmm," Clara assented from on high.

Despite her disapproval, the chickens had endured cramped quarters in a corner of the woodshed for far too long, and the structure would also house rabbits and provide a place for hay storage.

But the demands of the building project, which would be followed rapidly by gardening season, conflicted with my deep desire to write. Jay kept, at best, a cool distance from the fact that my career was blossoming, and even bearing fruit.

*Country Journal* had accepted my garden journal and had sent me a cheque for five hundred dollars American for the first instalment. It was scheduled to run throughout 1991. And to top it off, I had heard back from both of the American publishers I had contacted. Houghton Mifflin in Boston had asked to see my novel *Ningunsaw*, while Lyons and Burford in New York had requested an outline and sample material for a nonfiction account of wilderness life. But when could I possibly attend to these matters?

A sombre wind harassed the alder branches as Natalia and I helped Jay move logs over to the new barn site. As my body toiled, my mind teemed, silently contorting in an effort to figure out how to write a book about my experiences as a wilderness mother and make it interesting enough. I didn't dare share this dilemma with my husband. When he had a project going, nothing else existed. Lately the primary theme was the new barn. In the mornings while the snow was still hard, Jay had been hauling rounds of wood for shakes from the forest south of the garden. Then he had been spending the rest of the day splitting shakes. He had done about a thousand and figured he'd need close to two thousand. With the lengthening days, he had been pushing himself too hard and, as a result, was in a sour mood.

Now this morning Jay loaded the logs, one by one, onto the heavy homemade sled, a grim expression on his face. While Nat pushed her ten-year-old body against the sled, I steadied the log from behind. Then with the peavey and his back, Jay hoisted the brutes on board. Fastening a bungy cord around the front end, he then pulled while I pushed from the back, and Natty stayed by the sled and kept it on track. I knew I couldn't budge the bruisers without Jay. Once on track, the logs slid swiftly down the slope, flattening any saplings in their path. Most often I was on my knees, while a hardy push left me sprawled on the ground behind the rocketing sled.

A hefty pine log had to be retrieved from the sunny bench above the house. Jay stood astride and shouted down to me. "Bring the sled up here!" Pushing the hand-hewn tank up the sheer cement-hard hill was a real ordeal. My face soon matched my crimson coveralls.

"Bring it right over here to the log," he ordered. At the prospect of more distance to negotiate, I lost my cool.

"You might find it easy, but it's bloody hard for me to get this hog up the hill!"

Once the log was loaded, Natalia and I began pushing the sled. Jay instructed, "Now bring the sled down, and don't let go of it or it'll crack up! And bring the peavey!"

Awkwardly I held the weight back with one arm while I carried the tool with the other. Grip gone, I cursed twice in increasing volume as the peavey crashed down on my head.

With relief I rushed inside to prepare a lunch of moose soup and biscuits, then dashed back outside to peel logs for the new structure. Whenever Jay was in high gear, he expected everyone else to follow suit.

That night, a wolf crept in and ate one third of a mouldy bear hide that was tacked on the wheelhouse door, but I was so exhausted I slept soundly, oblivious to what was happening in the waking world.

The next morning, after assigning school work to both children, I helped Jay put logs in place. Each weighed at least three hundred pounds, and I mainly rolled and held the bruisers, manoeuvring them with the peavey squarely onto the end logs. Next I held them as Jay lifted up the butt end, then balanced them on a slab so they could be rolled over to where the foundation logs were notched together. Rather than notch the full length, he rough-notched the ends, then flipped them into place.

Later when the snow melted, the children and I took numerous excursions to gather moss for chinking, while Jay continued to hand-split shakes. Of the twelve twenty-foot logs required, I peeled ten. I genuinely enjoyed working outdoors, but the demands of perpetual cooking, baking, and home schooling, as well as numerous other chores, put pressure on me. And where was my precious writing time, which was supposed to extend at least from October until April? The strenuous outdoor work left me too weary to follow my early rising regime. I felt somehow that my writing career was being sabotaged, yet how could I flaunt its significance in the face of our physical need for better housing for the animals that provided us with eggs and meat? When it came to survival, there could be no arguing the point that these other projects took precedence. And as the years wore on and communication with Jay became more difficult, I began to protect myself by simply refraining from discussing these matters with him at all. He had accused me often of "only caring about my writing."

The arrival of the weekends and, on Sunday, the Handels brought relief from the tension and the back-breaking work. By the middle of January Gilbert had left his Aunt Bertha's place in Iskut Village to live with his family and so was a regular Sunday visitor. He had grown to be a good-looking young man with his luminous green eyes and deep dimples. His usually level head was tempered with flashes of creativity.

As much as Gilbert respected his father for his wisdom and talents, he looked down on his mother for her lack of it. Through characteristically clenched teeth, he would sum up Clara's education with the following: "They sent her home. They couldn't teach her nothing."

He had heard the story of how the nuns at the school in Telegraph Creek had grown impatient with Clara and had ordered her out. Yet as an unsympathetic preteen, he couldn't resist picking on her. Natalia had once discovered him outside the Handel hut, doctoring a container of his mom's snuff with cocoa, instant coffee, garlic powder, molasses, and cayenne. Later, when he asked her how it was, Clara unwittingly came out on top when she replied, "Dat's good. Ike dat nuff."

But because of Clara's compliance, which ran parallel to her streak of bear blood, Gilbert could smooth talk his mother out of her moosehide mittens, out of the new day pack we had given her for Christmas, out of the shirt off her back, out of the boots off her feet.

One day, when she arrived at my door, I squinted down at her boots.

"Clara! Where's your good boots?" Scuffing her way up the steps, her mouth sagged at the corners and a parade of self-pity passed through her eyes. "Gil BERT. Gil BERT DAN! He took dem!"

I dried my hands, wet from washing dishes, and indignantly voiced my support. "He has no right to do that, Clara! You should make him give them back!"

Staring at me intently, Clara nodded, then blurted out: "Dee ah

NAH, tink Gil BERT should give dem boots back?"

"That's for sure, Clara," I replied.

That day, as we flowed through the garden and the chores, through the steps of preparing lunch, my friend repeated the question. With frequent forays off into the ethics of it all, and why it wasn't doing Gilbert any good, I assured her that yes, he should give them back.

After lunch the four children, including Gilbert, sporting Clara's boots and dodging my dirty looks, wandered with us to Willow Park. We scampered across the snow crust like squirrels while all around the woods reverberated with the sounds of reuniting songbirds. The white snowpack between the trees was riddled with moose tracks. In the meadow, some of the willow saplings were chewed down to stubs. Others were missing large chunks of bark, and the moist paleness of the inner bark gleamed in the afternoon air. Here and there tufts of hair, snatched by branches as the moose browsed through, swung in the breeze. Fresh droppings, perfect ovals of varnished brown, gemmed the snow. Near Natty Creek, jumbo pussy willows grew at the top of chartreuse stalks. Their flamboyance shouted spring!

Willow Park had flooded, then frozen into a natural skating rink. We hadn't brought skates, but at Natalia's initiative we were soon playing a network of games across its glittering surface. When it came to charades, Clara imitated the person before her. When it came to "Go Go Stop," she was always the last to move. Her own children grew impatient and prodded her on with jeers.

"Clara, you dummy!" Julie chided. Despite her daughter's own limitations, adolescence, with its built-in parent rejecter, was kicking in.

Clara didn't retort, but failure flickered through her eyes as she silently watched us. In a chance meeting with a nurse from Telegraph Creek, I had learned that, as was commonly the case in those days, Clara's condition had never been diagnosed. Somewhere in her psyche, though, Clara knew that she wasn't "normal." My heart went out to her because I had suffered throughout life from my own inability to fit in, and I knew the sting of rejection. She must have wondered if she would ever be able to communicate. In another sense she had the same struggles as everyone else. For even with the gift of wordflow, the possibility of being misunderstood is always present. Filtered through the ears of the listener, personal beliefs and biases censor certain phrases while others are twisted or amplified. Or tossed aside in favour of hidden meanings that may or may not lurk beneath the rocks.

With my own children I was learning that plain talk and repetition were the most effective ways of getting my meaning across. Clara was good at plain talk. It was just that none of her words seemed ordinary because of the labour involved in birthing them into the darkness of the world, into the light of day. And Clara did feel loneliness. It revealed itself in slumped shoulders, a hard-set countenance, and a spine determined to hold the phantoms of rejection at bay. She accepted the risk of drawing close to others, like a frightened foreigner surrounded by mother tongues babbling incessantly and senselessly on without her.

Soon enough we wound our way back through the forest to the cosy kitchen. As we entered, the aroma of roasting rabbit wafted across from the Findlay oval cookstove. Fritz sat on the broad step leading up to the main room, relaxing after helping Jay rig up an electric grain grinder. Crossing his long legs, he nodded a greeting. Each Sunday I looked forward to the chance to converse with him. Most often it was the Jay-Fritz team and the Deanna-Clara team.

I just finished reading *Deschooling Society* by Ivan Illich," I said.

"I find Illich kind of obscure at times," Fritz replied, craning his neck from side to side in an attempt to see around his wife. Clara had the most annoying habit of positioning her body right between us whenever we tried to carry on a conversation. It was one of her ways of getting attention, but we talked around her.

When Clara finally wandered off, I sank into the corner of the kitchen bench. "Yeah, Illich loses me, but here and there his writing has flashes of brilliance."

When Fritz listened to me he did so without making eye contact. Instead, leaning his elbows on his knees and clasping his hands loosely, his eyes remained on the floor while he concentrated fully on my words. We rambled through fields of philosophy, psychology, and social comment.

"Jay is reading *The Origin of the Species* by Charles Darwin right now," I mentioned. Fritz was soft-spoken and he chose his words with great care. His replies didn't come quickly, or with any trace of impatience or sarcasm. Rather the words emerged as measured beats of rationality.

I think the Darwinian perception of life is the most serious problem of our time," said Fritz. He went on to explain that it was the "survival of the fittest" aspect of Darwin's theory that he viewed as ultimately lethal. "If you believe in Darwinism, it becomes necessary to feel you are superior because the inferior are doomed to extinction. Darwinism taken to its logical conclusion produced the Holocaust." Shifting on the step, Fritz explained how at one time he had been a total believer in the survival of the fittest philosophy. So seduced was he by the spirit of competition, he had begun to lose compassion for humanity. The Vietnam war and life with Clara and Julie had presented him with another perspective. With quiet conviction, Fritz repeated his belief that Darwin's theory of evolution was one of the most destructive ideas embraced by our society.

"And the whole educational system operates by this same principle."

We spoke often of education, and its true meaning, and the corruption of the term by the modern system. My role as home instructor had compelled me to closely examine this issue. In the Handel household, it was up to Fritz. Gilbert had tried school up at Iskut

Village but it had felt like a stifling prison to him. He tiptoed around the territory of the written word, but from his father he had inherited solid mechanical ability and common sense. Julie was still struggling to learn to read and write, but she was keen enough to pursue it independently to some degree. It was a simple case of letting interest take the lead in learning.

Fritz had arrived at the realization that nature has evolved through co-operation rather than competition. I found his presence calming and I trusted him. I looked forward to the time each Sunday when we could share ideas.

Glowing from the outing to Willow Park, Clara perched on the sealskin-topped barrel and, with a plug of chewing tobacco in her cheek, tipped a box containing a jigsaw puzzle onto the table. It seemed a marvel that Clara could do puzzles. I was a complete idiot when it came to interlocking random shapes. Frowning, she would study the bits, then with fingers that failed at sewing but could make bannock, she locked the edges together. She made quick work of the centre, which filled up with a picture of Donald Duck. I wondered, is she smarter than me, as victoriously she slapped the last piece into place. With a manner still humble, despite the glimmer of satisfaction in her black eyes, she sought, then received, my genuine admiration.

In so many ways I had come to enjoy, even cherish, my time with Clara, but one of the times I *didn't* appreciate Clara's company was when I went up to my desk. There, at the top of the stairs, I entered my haven.

If there was any portion of the property that I felt was mine, this was it. Midst the camouflage of visiting day commotion, still wearing my dump apron that read, "Got more time for misbehavin' since I started microwavin'," I sped up the unpainted stairs. At the top I basked in the light from the window that framed South Mountain. Below it sat my desk, its surface of tropical wood shining. Bookshelves, with all of my favourites, including *Fool's Progress* by Edward Abbey, *Under*

*Milkwood* by Dylan Thomas, *Writing Down the Bones* by Natalie Goldberg, and *Pilgrim at Tinker Creek* by Annie Dillard, lined the left wall. From the shelf underneath, I pulled a bulky manuscript, which I quietly placed on my desk. As I nervously flipped through the pages, Clara drew up beside me and released a deep sigh. When she followed me there, she entered a territory in which she would never feel at home. My compulsion to scribble endless circles onto paper was an enigma for Clara. While she could not relate to a single written word, for me it was a vital part of my life and also a strategy for survival. No matter how painful my experiences became, as long as I could write I could cope, make sense of seemingly random events, and even rise above the occasional agony of being alive. Despite the income generated it was an activity that was, most often, discouraged. Jay had once summed it up with, "If you got one book out you'd just want to go on and write another book! And another book! And another book!" Clearly he saw my passion as nothing more than a hopeless addiction.

Clara soon went back down the stairs to check the potato pot, which was rumbling on the stove. Anxious to get *Ningunsaw*, my attempt at a novel, off to Houghton Mifflin, my aim was to check to make sure that every one of the 653 pages was there. Clara couldn't stay away from me for long, and soon she was back upstairs. She came to a halt beside me, her hands planted firmly on her hips. I could imagine the tedium of watching someone flip through a mound of papers, particularly when there was no apparent reason.

With growing amazement I realized that even after page fifty, she was still with me. One hundred flew by and she still stood her ground. As I followed the sequence through to 500, 600, and finally 653, my buddy still stood solidly and stared hard at the blur of paper. Even though she couldn't read a single word, she was committed to seeing the task through with me.

It wasn't until years later that I truly recognized the potency of the support emanating from her at that time. Even though Clara was incapable of ever understanding the obscure symbols, what she did understand was how important it was to me. Clara's presence that day clearly conveyed, without words, the depth of her friendship and devotion.

For weeks I didn't wander beyond the Ningunsaw Valley, and Clara was usually by my side. As she walked behind me I flashed back to the beginning of our friendship. When I first met her, I didn't know what to make of her. She seemed a baffling blend of complete idiocy, ancient wisdom, childlike mirth, and angry woman. As the months wore on I recognized that she was just the same as the rest of us. She simply had different proportions of the same ingredients. As the only two women in the valley we shared our simple pleasures in life, and also our frustrations. Our frustrations with children, endless chores, and, yes, husbands.

Clara clomped behind me in plaid flannel shirt, jeans, and Gilbert's boots, her hair in the French braid I had fashioned that afternoon. The snow was slow to go, but the hills flanking the trail leading north were revealing their moss. Crossbills flitted along Natty Creek, and on the opposite side of the trail we passed a conglomeration of rock I called Broodgloom, which provided a lookout post for porcupine, wolf, and moose.

When we crossed a small freshet that fingered the forest's depths, Clara called out, "HI WATER!" and stood waving to the garrulous stream. I released a chuckle. When she turned, her face was etched with hurt.

"Why you laugh?"

"I don't know," I shrugged sheepishly. "Why did I laugh? The stream is alive." Turning to face each direction, I sang out my greeting, "Hi, water! Hi, sky! Hi, trees! Hi, Earth!" Beside me, the grandmother living within Clara grinned brightly.

Suddenly overcome with the burden I was carrying, I sank to a log and my buddy plunked down beside me. Because we were alone and she was my friend, I poured my heart out to her. I spoke of the agony of turning myself inside out to please a man. "He thinks I don't share his philosophies at all. I realize how vital self-sufficiency is and it can only become more so. I see all of this, Clara, and I know how ridiculous it is to transport food thousands of miles, burning more fossil fuels in the process, when it's possible to grow a better product right in our own backyard." I paused and looked at Clara. She was staring intently at me, taking in every word.

"I'll tell you one major difference between Jay and me. I still want to be connected to the rest of the human race. Right now my pen connects me with the outside world and I feel good about the income it brings in. But my reason for writing has never been to get rich. It's deeper than that. Even when I lived out in civilization, I never worked in order to own a bunch of things. I used my money to broaden my experience, to travel.

"Believe me, I've thought more than once of leaving Jay but I stay for many reasons. For one thing I recognize in what a perilous place our planet is and how important our way of life is here. I'm not naïve enough to think I can see into the future, but I understand that the greenhouse effect alone is going to bring catastrophic consequences. Did you know that, Clara?"

She nodded soberly and I continued, "And it's all due to human activity, like the massive burning of fossil fuels and the clear-cutting of our forests. The earth's temperature is rising, the sea levels are rising. We could be facing environmental refugees in the future, displaced by floods, droughts, and famine."

I knew I was talking over her head but her attention was so genuine, her support so palpable that I felt I could let the dam burst. She was my friend, and sometimes friends just listened. "What needs to change is our pattern of perpetually wielding power over nature, of trying to dominate and control it, as though it's something separate and outside of ourselves. If we experienced the earth as part of ourselves, this wouldn't be possible because it would mean brutalizing and destroying ourselves in the process. The earth is a living breathing being and we need to acknowledge and honour our relationship with her. You know that, Clara. You greeted the water along the trail and at first I even laughed.

"Do you see how lethal that attitude is, Clara? What humans have done to the planet in the past two hundred years has also been done, historically, to women. There's no sane reason for men to wield power over the heads of women, for Jay to demand that I do his bidding. Unless a balance is achieved between masculine and feminine power, there's no hope for humans on this planet." I paused and stared up at a red squirrel sassing us from a balsam branch, then went on, "I have endured Jay's attitude because this has been my dream too. Twelve years of my life have also gone into our home and we have learned to survive out here. But I see no reason why our dream of independence can't co-exist with my writing dream. To tell you the truth, the bond that has grown between me and this valley has been strong enough, deep enough, and rich enough to keep me here, despite the way he's treated me. I'm willing to acknowledge that I need him. Yet he makes me feel so terrible."

My friend listened without judging, and her face crumpled as I dissolved into tears. Throwing her arms around me, she wailed, "Don worry, Dee ah NAH! You good woman. I like you Dee ah NAH!"

The compassion that flowed with her tears was astounding. As a shaft of sunlight ignited an intricacy of hidden bark and branches it occurred to me that if depth of feeling were any measure of intelligence, then Clara was a genius.

# *Bear Awakening*

S norting fiercely, Clara trudged behind me through thigh-deep snow, to the bowl of wooded land cradled between hills. At this elevation the snow was slower to go. Our destination lay halfway between the Ningunsaw Valley homestead and Desiré Lake, where Natalia had been born. I stared up at the swaying branches and felt the flicker of tiny snowflakes melting on my warm face.

The mute pearl sky was brightened by the solitary piping of a whisky jack, grey jay, or camp robber. The full-feathered bird on the pine branch answered to none of the names given by humans. At our feet the snow was scattered with pinecone petals from the frantic feeding of red squirrels. With shocked tails, they scolded us from an ever higher branch as we passed. Midst the ceaseless chatter I heard the message to prepare for the future. But I never was prepared for the scene that lay just beyond the hem of living breathing trees.

Even entombed in snow, the clear-cut articulated a harsh statement about human arrogance. An elaborate ecosystem that had once flowed uninterrupted to the end of the horizon had been annihilated. Cut to the core. A brisk north wind now scoured the cut-block, the butcher's block, and enveloped us. It was like a blast of poison to my being. Did Clara feel it too—exposed, unprotected by the foliage to which we both belonged? I shook my head in despair.

"They just don't know, Clara. They just don't know how much our souls shrink with each falling forest."

Beside me Clara placed her hands on her hips and, slouching slightly, regarded me with black sparkling eyes. Taking a pinch of Copenhagen, she nodded in sympathy. "Him don't know. No good dem take dem woods."

As we turned, the moist sadness of the remaining forest encompassed us. Instinctively I put my hands on the shaggy bark of a white birch and felt the energy, simultaneously grounding and celestial. The tree was a wand. It swayed between the slip-away edge of a steep hill and the ever changing spirit of the sky.

"I love these woods, Clara," I said with conviction. "I've known them, moved through them for over a decade. I've led a lonely life, and the forest has been my community. In the beginning other people seldom walked here. And when they finally did arrive, they came to destroy what they found."

Clara's eyes hardened as she stammered, "Should tell 'im FU KOFF asshole! Right Dee ah NAH?"

"Right on, Clara."

Leading her home I felt the silken silence of the woods permeate my being and restore my peace. It was a special silence entwined with the song of the wind and the multilingual voice of the land. We both used sticks for support in the collapsing snow. Abruptly I stopped, a trifle confused. "Isn't it strange, Clara? I can find my path through the trees, but when they take them all away I almost feel lost." My friend nodded her head soberly in agreement.

Near a brooding boulder I turned and waited for Clara to catch up. She was staring straight up at the treetops as she stumbled along. I was astounded by her face, which was lit by nothing less than ecstasy. At that moment I saw for the first time the love that was chan-

nelled through the little bent branch of a body. She walked transformed behind me.

One month later I also saw the fear that could seize her like a leaf
in a March wind. The outing began serenely enough. Clara, with her
fists clenched and as fit as a fox, followed my footsteps while Julie
loped lank-haired behind.

I was spellbound by the rebirth of the forest. Violets bloomed
amidst ferns so delicate they could scarcely tolerate human touch.

"Oh look! There's a lady's slipper!" Without hesitation I dropped
to my knees for a drink of the exotic perfume. Glancing up from the
exquisite purple shoe, offset with a small fan of petals, I invited Clara
and Julie to bend and smell it.

With her nose nearly sucking up the source of the ephemeral
sweetness, Clara inhaled briskly. Next Julie dropped to the ground
and, taking a sample sniff, followed it with a nod of agreement.

We soon came to South Bend. This jog in the river trail was sur-
veyed from both sides by swarthy cottonwood sentinels. The wind
was predictably from the southwest. There icefields stretched one
hundred miles to the Pacific Ocean, while above us the breeze held
the freshly hatched splendour of new leaves. I had read with enthusiasm how many native tribes viewed the cottonwood with reverence.
Some even believed that if a troubled person sat in the shadow of one
of these giants, the tree would offer counsel. *CRACK.* We all froze at
the sharp sound from the woods to the west. The snap announced
the presence of what could only have been a moose or bear. Stricken
with fear, Julie's face blanched while Clara sucked her mouth in far
from sight. My palms sweated, my mind raced.

"We're going to have to make some noise to let it know we're
here. The worst thing would be to surprise it. Hey, bear!" I shouted.
"You better STAY AWAY!"

While I put forth a bold front, Clara and Julie stood limply,
unable to find their voices. My heart felt like a sparrow, frantic for

freedom from my chest. Having been charged once by a black bear in the garden, I knew firsthand how unpredictable these creatures were, and I respected them immensely.

After an endless moment, my companions came through with a trickle of voice power.

"Don bodder us, bear," Clara called. As time ticked away no black ball of fur emerged from the foliage.

My courage returning, I began to gather horsetails for the goslings. The other two followed suit, even though I knew Clara had mixed feelings about geese. She understood that these tweetering fluff-balls sometimes turned into terrible ganders, like Gandhi, who with his neck snaking out menacingly and on nude pink feet, rocked across the yard after Clara every time she ventured to visit. Latching onto her butt or thigh, he pinched her without mercy.

"Dat dam goose! Him al ways bite me!" Clara would complain. Yet her voice held a trace of acceptance.

What I learned from Clara that day in the woods was how to be resilient in the face of adversity. And this was not because Clara was resilient. Rather, she served as a mirror. Her knocking knees at the prospect of a bear reflected back my own fear. By being able to see it in her, I could measure the excess in my own reaction. At the same time I could empathize because I had known fear from the inside out, had travelled down its siren throat and cowered in its chartreuse belly.

Slowly we wound our way home through a shifting veil of spruce and balsam branches, resplendent with bright born tips. The whole world seemed fresh and tender. The first squadron of mosquitoes had dispersed and we were enjoying the lull before the storm. Emerging from the trees, my eyes feasted on hundreds of scarlet and golden tulips, stretching in ribbons from east to west across the garden.

Despite the rapture of spring, this was also the season when the possibility of bear kept us on our toes. It loomed behind every moss-shrouded log, beside each unearthed root system—webs linking the micro-organisms of soil and tree. And the boundaries of our clearing meant nothing to the bruin who had dwelled there for eons.

One morning, as Nat was leaving the outhouse, Spooky, our unkempt terrier, broke into what was clearly a bear bark and tore out of the building and east. Less than thirty feet away, on the same slope, stood a hefty black bear.

Caught up in her barking frenzy, Spooky abandoned all caution. She braced herself less than two feet from the beast, who observed her with beady eyes at the base of a prominent snout. More curious than afraid, Nat lingered in the doorway and watched. Luckily, the bulky bear simply sat there, since one cuff could have sent Spooky to the next world. Finally, the bear wandered away, round-rumped and swinging its nose from side to side.

Later, Ben and Jay strolled down to the German cabin only to discover two bears in the yard. One clambered for the heights of a nearby spruce tree while the other tore for the base of the hill.

First cautioning Ben to stay back, Jay snatched rocks from nearby and advanced toward the bear still on the ground. In a big voice, Ben hollered, "Don't chase that bear! You're crazy!" At the same instant Jay hit the furry beast in the side. It dashed away.

The following Sunday the Handels were late. We pondered, had they forgotten the day or were they dealing with problem bears? It proved to be the latter.

Finally around 2:00 P.M. the four of them trooped in. Fritz was bent under the weight of a camouflage-coloured pack full of bear meat. Close behind trudged Clara, and with an air of fatigue, yet importance, she drew a container of cleaned intestine and one of bear liver out of her pack. Slamming them down, she splattered the counter, wall, window, and her own face with blood. Moments later, when Jay came into the house, she had to repeat the performance. Each time I jumped and wondered, was she mad at someone?

It was a challenge to get a straight story out of the Handel crew.

Finally, with his green eyes flashing and in a voice nearly annihilated by clenched teeth, Gilbert explained.

"He was a real nuisance bear. He kept hangin' around, even ripped holes in my window. Tore the plastic." Reluctant to resort to a rifle, Fritz had discharged a bear banger, a small explosive device designed to simply scare bears away. Uncannily, the device had issued no noise at all, and rather than sailing in the direction of the bear, it had landed two feet behind Fritz.

"Don't put too much faith in them," he advised, raising his arched eyebrows.

Briefly the bear had retreated. Just moments later, as Gilbert climbed the steep wooded incline to the clear-cut, the bruin re-emerged and stood between the boy and his father. As Gilbert tried to sidle past him to Fritz, the bear, with powerful limbs, advanced toward him. The bear refused to budge from the vicinity. Finally, Fritz felt there was no choice but to shoot it. By the small hours of the morning the beast was butchered. The whole Handel family trooped into our place smelling of the scene.

Fritz and Jay spent the rest of Sunday chatting while they cut up the meat. As always, the bones were boiled down for soup stock, and most of the meat was made into sausage, using the intestine for casing.

As spring unfolded, the days were crammed with outdoor work and I helped outside as much as I could between home schooling, baking, laundry, meals, and maintaining household order.

In the far field I raked up dead grass to use for mulch, then bustled back up to the yard to sort and stack the wood left over from shake splitting. Back in the garden I spent hours packing down broad patches of wheat and experimental grain, bounding over them with bare feet. Natalia and Ben joined in whenever it looked like fun. But when I lugged buckets of leaf mould over the log bridge, my children were nowhere in sight. On the opposite side of Natty Creek, I had sifted the decaying leaves through frames covered with wire mesh. Once across the bridge, I sprinkled the fibres over freshly planted rows of celery, celeriac, and broad beans.

Gathering buckets of clover for the rabbits was a daily chore and usually at least one child came along to help. One morning Ben was glad he did. As we fed a grey doe called Stubborn, Spooky suddenly sprang south across the clearing. Glancing beyond the garden I caught sight of a lanky black wolf gliding along the edge of the forest. Ben was struck speechless while Spooky kept up her barking solo for half an hour.

As the days stretched out and claimed more and more territory from the darkness, Jay dug trenches in the far garden and placed the seed potatoes in them. Behind him I raked all eleven one-hundred-foot rows closed, burying the spuds and smoothing the surface. Meanwhile the ruffed grouse beat its feathers to a blur, and Natalia crawled close to its drumming spot beneath a branchy balsam and met the alarmed eye of the bird.

One breezy afternoon I was summoned to help carry several weather-laden logs from near the barn across the footbridge spanning Natty Creek. The aim was to line the far side of the creek with them so that the geese couldn't gain entry to the garden. With red beret cocked at an impatient angle, and heedless of what was happening at my end, Jay charged ahead. I toiled to keep up but my feet became tangled in the long matted grass and elderberry canes. It was all I could do to hold the massive log and keep my legs moving at the same time. No matter how I pushed myself, I could not keep up with Jay.

One morning I had been sitting at my desk for a few minutes only to hear him stamp his way up the stairs and ask how much longer I planned to write. Later downstairs he served an ultimatum. I was to put all of my writing away by March 21, or go to see a lawyer about a divorce.

"What if I get a contract for a book?" I asked tremulously.

He replied that I would have to find somewhere else to write it.

A few days later he softened and said I should pick two days out of the week to write. Then abruptly he changed his mind again.

On June 20, as I whipped up a lemon chiffon cake for Natalia's eleventh birthday, I heard the Whitehorse operator call out our number through the undulating static of the radiophone. As I answered, a distant voice asked for Diane Kawatski. Ignoring the error, I said, "Speaking," and the voice returned, "Amazing." It was Karen Bokram, the editor of *Mother Earth News* magazine, calling from New York. Not only did they want permission to reprint my article of "Living the Dream," they were also requesting further work.

Within a couple of days, along with the rest of the mail, Jay packed in a letter from Peter Burford in New York requesting two sample chapters and a complete contents of *Wilderness Mother*. On the basis of this material, Burford would make his final decision about the book.

Never had prospects looked brighter, yet how was I to accomplish this when my literary attempts were met with fluctuating degrees of coldness? Regularly Jay reminded me that he had once been editor of his school newspaper in Wisconsin. He wanted me to grant him permission to take a pencil to my work. I refused and retreated into my shell and curled around my literary creations in an attitude of complete protection. In the meantime, besides the demands of gardening, we were busy digging up ground in the front yard, removing rocks and throwing them into the trenches that Jay had dug for walkways.

More than ever the arrival of each weekend brought relief from the tension. The next Sunday I invited the Handels on an outing to the river. Natalia, who had been rude to Gilbert, was left behind, but Ben, Gilbert, and Julie followed while Clara brought up the rear. Jay was too busy in the garden to take a break, but Fritz promised to follow later.

The walk to the river, deep beneath the crowns of spruce and cottonwood, was inevitably a humbling experience. The main channel of the Ningunsaw River was both high and wide, a murky watered beast that stripped away the definition of bank and hurled whole trees down its belly. The river changed its course with erratic delight, constantly carving out new paths, then abandoning them in favour of yet another low-lying reach. Beyond the racing jade waters, the luminous peaks of the Coast Mountains scaled an opaline sky.

Abruptly we came to a halt at a knee-deep side stream, which blocked our path toward an inviting stretch of black sand. Plunking down, I tore off my boots and rolled up my pants. Meanwhile Gilbert and Ben, in a flurry, ripped off their clothes and, giggling, pranced naked through the sparkling water. Reaching the coveted sand, they rolled until they both wore a coat of it. Julie laughed loudly and stumbled barefoot after them. However Clara, who had revealed small dainty feet beneath the swaddling of socks, was afraid to cross the channel. Standing astride, her face crumpled at the sight of the shallow, yet swirling water.

Ben, sensing trouble on the far side, plunged into the current and scampered across, shedding his coat of sand. He romped up to Clara, who stood stranded on her own island of apprehension.

"I'll help you, Clara."

"Mm hmmm," she replied, and with full trust she took the small hand he extended. Even though the water posed no real threat, Clara was afraid and Ben came through with compassion. I will never forget the sight of my five-year-old son, wearing only his cap of flaxen hair, and scarcely rising to Clara's waist, leading the spindly woman to supposed safety on the opposite side. He slowed his pale limbs to accommodate her stumbling gait across a streambed made uneven by a mosaic of rocks.

An hour later Fritz found us. For a spell we all wandered around with our noses to the ground in search of intriguing rocks. Fritz, in

his usual red-and-black plaid wool coat, walked slowly and thought-
fully. At last perching on a cottonwood log, he studied his specimens,
cracking the odd stone apart to examine the centre.

As I plucked grey potato-shaped rocks and black egg-shaped rocks,
so satisfying in their solidity, from the shore, my mood plunged. For
they reminded me of the stone growing in my own chest. A growth
caused by grief and the suppression of my spirit.

Having no desire to burden Fritz with the details of my marital
strife, I wandered west. After all, he had his own relationship with Jay,
and if I confided in him, he would possibly end up in the middle of
the mess. I was soon swallowed by a grove of aromatic cottonwood
and the incantations of the Ningunsaw. I sank to the shore and brooded.
I had dealt with these difficulties alone so far and perhaps that was
the way it had to be. Maybe I had to simply accept the fact that I
would never experience appreciation or any type of validation in
this marriage. Instead I would watch my inner light fade to a mere
flicker.

Without warning, a twig snapped behind me. Spinning around, I
saw Clara creeping through the maze of branches.

"Whatsa matter, Dee ah NAH?" At the sight of my weathered little
friend, with her straggly black hair, I stood up. I'm certain my face
was full of despair. I told her about Jay's ultimatum.

Clara listened, her eyes glittering like black obsidian. With glossy
lips turned distinctly down at the corners, she stood astride and pressed
two tiny tapered index fingers together with a fierce intensity. Holding them in front of her face, she wrestled out the words. When they
at last emerged, it was from somewhere deep within, in a long forgotten cave of primal knowing. Her black hair swayed in the breeze, like
moss in an ancient forest, and she began to speak, her voice resonant
like a woodwind instrument and only a whisper.

"Why don't you. . . ?" Her voice then rose, like a stampede of horses,
gathering speed, furious hoof beats echoing against canyon walls. At

the same time that she shouted, "SPL IT UP?" she tore her fingers away from each other in wide arcs in opposite directions. As entertaining as the gesture was, it was also a call to freedom. It ignited wings in my ribcage. It mesmerized me, showed me what I didn't often dare to think about. With the tight intimacy of her fingers torn apart, they were suddenly free to soar in their separate directions. Deep in my heart I knew that Clara's weird pantomime held the power of a prophecy.

# Friends on the Hill

The passage of time revealed itself in new glints of grey in Clara's ebony hair. And I jolted at the sight of coarse white sprouts in my own dark mane. It was a full year later, in the spring of 1992. We roamed a ridge together while far below us the Ningunsaw River wound through a blush of new leaves. On the edge of a cliff a congregation of butterflies exploded in the warm sun, while a warbler landed on a fallen pine branch.

Lured to a resting spot on a sunny knoll, I sat down, then patted the ground, inviting Clara to sit beside me. With a small groan she bent to take her place on the moss. Her leathery face was creased with humour and humility. The fact that she left little space between us didn't bother me anymore. Perched on the brow of the hill together, we sat for an endless moment saying nothing. Instead we shared in the silence of the north, the coming and going of the Ice Age, the pain of being alive. While mountains rose and sank and the hill hummed ever so softly beneath us, I felt the edges of my personal boundaries give way.

With time Clara and I had merged as womanspirit. Members of the same mysterious clan. With each passing instant we moved farther away from our own birthing moments, from our moments of being born. We shared our own insignificance in the big picture, and the small one as well, where a man's opinion carried so much more weight than a woman's.

The wind set the pine needles shivering, and time was marked by the deep footprints of wolves, who followed their impulses upstream, then down, in winter and spring.

Twisting around, Clara put her dainty hand into the deep depression of an animal track. "Wofe," she uttered. We were in the river of wolf flow, its course marked by the presence of scat and tracks. Close by was a cluster of perfect oval moose droppings.

"Dat moose," Clara proclaimed.

"It sure is. Clara, do you see where the river disappears around the corner? " She craned her neck and gazed in the direction I indicated. "There's a canyon down there. A few winters back Jay had quite an experience there. Want to hear the story?"

"Mm hmm," Clara nodded, digging the heels of her gumboots into the bank, and, with her mouth slightly agape, preparing to listen. Toying with a pine cone, I began.

"It happened one spring when Jay was tearing up the Ningunsaw River on the snowmobile, breaking trail to haul in supplies. First he saw fresh tracks, then veering around a sharp bend just before the canyon, he caught sight of a cow moose running for its life. Right on its heels were two timber wolves. Hearing the whine of the snowmobile, the smaller grey one bolted for the forest. But the big cream-coloured guy was so obsessed with the hunt it didn't seem to notice the machine gaining on it. The moose's left front leg was already damaged, and over and over again the wolf leaped and tore at the open wound. Jay was only two hundred feet away when the long-legged moose suddenly lost its footing on the ice and fell onto its belly."

"Bang!" Clara shouted, driving her fist into an open hand for effect. Encouraged by her attentiveness, I continued.

"Never in all of his years in the bush had Jay witnessed such a struggle. I couldn't believe what happened next. In a flash the large wolf was on the moose's back. The cow frantically regained its footing and fled downstream. Bucking like a wild bronco, it finally managed to throw its enemy, which landed, with a thump, flat out in the snow. I went up to the canyon the next day and saw the amazing imprint of the wolf in the snow, the blood, and the story in the tracks.

"The poor moose struggled on. With the smell of its own death in its nostrils, and the pain in its leg blotting out the cold, the cow wobbled through the canyon. Tough as hell, the wolf bounced up again and sped after the cow, snapping at its heavy heels. On the far side of the canyon the moose turned to stare at Jay advancing on his machine. The wolf, with remarkable yellow eyes set in a black mask, whirled around and saw him for the first time. After a cold stare, it fled into the woods on the south side of the river. Meanwhile, the wounded moose dragged itself to an alder thicket on the opposite shore and collapsed."

Clara's face was infused with fire as she spat out, "Dat dam wofe!"

"Don't blame the wolves, Clara," I said, while the black pebble eyes explored my face. "It's nature's way. There've been a couple of times I could have died on the river and it had nothing to do with wolves."

"You?"

"Yeah. Two years ago, I had a stupid accident. I was climbing on a chair to get a flashlight from the shelf. The chair tipped backward and I fell on my right leg. I had already twisted my right knee at least three times before and the ligaments aren't what they used to be. The pain was so terrible I didn't even remember bumping my head. I screamed and Jay carted me to the couch and plunked me there while Christoph, who was staying with us, ran to get bags of snow. Jay doesn't have much patience with injuries and he told me I'd have to hop around and do as much as I could.

"Three days later my foot and ankle were still swollen tight and their colours could have rivalled the aurora borealis. They were green, blue, and dark purple where the ankle bone once was. And was it ever cold—below zero. Finally on February 14, a full five days after the accident, Jay bundled me and my crutches in a blanket on the sled. I had needed the crutches five years earlier when I'd hurt my knee the first time. You know how steep the hills are on our trail, and the river was the only level way to get out. Luckily Christoph was with us and could go back to stay with the kids. We hated to leave them alone, but there was no choice because someone had to take the sled and snowmobile home."

"Dem kids stay home?" Clara asked, planting her hands on her knees.

"Yup. Christoph rode at the back of the skinny sled while Jay towed us both upstream. He had me ride facing front so the weight would be toward the rear, and the snow kept stinging me like a swarm of bees. The sky was grey and snow devils were whirling across the river flat. As I hunkered down inside my parka, I wondered if we'd make it. The snowmobile kept bogging down in the waist-deep snow. Over and over again Jay had to stop the machine, and he and Chris wrestled with it to keep it moving. I knew that if we broke down we'd be in deep trouble. Even for a person with two good legs, walking without snowshoes would have been tough. For me it would have been impossible. By the time we finally reached the road I was vibrating from the first stages of hypothermia. And as my hands thawed the chilblains set in."

I watched a shiver of sympathy pass through Clara's frame. "What den?"

"Well, Christoph rushed back to Natalia and Ben while I crawled up the steep bank to the road. The stretch of highway at the base of Echo Lake hill was as nasty as ever. The wind whined through the trees and blasted us in the face. Jay was too cold to stand in one spot, and so I struggled along on my crutches behind him. As you know there's an average of a car an hour out there in winter.

"At last, with my spirits rising, I watched not one, but two cars approaching. Leaning on my crutches, I stuck my thumb out and watched amazed."

"How come?"

"Would you believe they both passed us by?"

"Asshole!" Clara growled.

"After what seemed like forever, while my ankle throbbed and I lost the feeling in my toes, a transport truck finally stopped. Four hours later, when we arrived at the Stewart hospital, I found out that I had broken the fibula bone in my ankle."

At the mention of the word hospital, Clara hoisted up her four shirts and displayed the purple scar on her abdomen. "Dat doctor cu cu cut me," she stammered.

Clara's longest time in a town of any size came after a gall bladder attack. Fritz had driven her down to Terrace, more than three hundred miles south. After checking her into the Mills Memorial Hospital, he had set up camp in the park, sleeping and eating in the tall brown box he had built on the back of his truck. Fritz was there for his wife before and after the operation. As Clara stammered through her story, I could only begin to imagine how traumatic it must have been for her. "It stink in dere," she grumbled. How she must have hated the glossy floors, bright lights, and antiseptic smell, when she was used to wood smoke, floors with a comfortable amount of grime, and sunshine through the small smudged window of her Iskut abode. But being Clara I could also imagine her barking out something outrageous, even obscene, which would crack the face of the most austere orderly. The purple scar left behind, after they had entered her body and snatched out the vile part, was more than an attention grabber. It was also a symbol of the horror and wonder of modern medicine, so radically different from the herbal remedies of her people.

"It must have been scary for you, Clara," I sympathized. She nodded gravely, then glanced over at my jeans, permanently stained from
garden work.

"How's your knee, Dee ah NAH? Hurtin?"

"Not too bad now," I replied, then launched into the story of how
five years earlier I had sprained my right knee badly for the second
time five thousand feet up South Mountain, on an overnight hike.
Pointing to the peak directly south of us on the far side of the
Ningunsaw, I described the accident, and how it had come at the end
of a beautiful day of walking the mountain ridges with Jay for miles,
and boot-skiing the permanent snow patches. My legs were already
worn out when we began our descent and I had sprained the knee
just after we entered the timber again. I had five thousand feet to
struggle down and a river to cross at the bottom.

"It was nearly straight up and down," I told Clara, "and I had to
hobble all the way down to the river. I was terrified about crossing the
water, but did I have any choice? Home and the kids were on the
other side. And wouldn't you know it? My worst nightmare came
true. The current grabbed Jay and I and started sweeping us downstream. For a long moment that I will never forget, I was convinced I
wouldn't see my kids again. Thank God we managed to grab onto the
opposite shore."

The drama combined with the mention of children triggered Clara's
memory of when her belly had been huge. She held her arms out
wide, as though encompassing a beach ball, to indicate her increased
circumference.

"Him cut me open, den take de baby out." With colossal effort,
she delivered the tale of what must have been one of the most intense
experiences of her life. Her face was clenched against the pain of remembering, recalling the violation of having masked and gloved strangers intrude upon the inner reaches of her body. She pondered the
memory and would have happily told the story over and over again.

And though stunted by fate, Clara was developed enough in the realm of relationships to always ask how it had been for me.

"You?" she asked, opening the door so that she could view the delivery of my children into the world.

"Nat was born at home. Jay delivered her. Ben was born in Stewart . . . and Jay wasn't there at all."

"Cha ay stay home?"

"Yeah. It was in December and he had to stay home to look after the animals and to keep the fires going so the canning didn't freeze."

Clara shifted, and in the process kicked a rock loose. It clattered its way down the gravel bluff toward the distant river while above us two sapsuckers whined, then landed on opposite sides of a pine tree. Their tap-tapping message rang out across the stillness.

"Cha ay. Him should kean his mess," Clara complained, shaking her head. From the outset she had expressed the opinion that Jay should be responsible for his own messes. This was noteworthy since my friend held few opinions.

At the mere mention of mate and mess, a tangle of unresolved conflicts rose up in me, but rather than release them in a tide of resentment, I decided to share a recent vision with my friend. It had been a source of power and reassurance. I was confident that she would listen without judging.

The afternoon was wearing on, and I yanked a pair of rabbit skin mittens, with one thumb worn thin, out of my pocket and pulled them on.

"Clara, last week when I was walking the path to your place I was feeling absolutely down. I truly wondered right then if I could cope with the pressures in my life. Just as I reached the upper bench where all of the birch trees grow, I flashed on this vision." I could feel Clara's body grow tense and alert beside me. "I saw an old native woman. She was naked besides a loincloth. She sat astride a shimmering nut-brown horse. The woman was scarred by life, and yet she was still strong and sinewy, with long silver hair and a flaming red headband. In her right hand she held a staff the colour of satiny dried cottonwood. From it trailed another long red scarf. The woman's face was set as she rode steadfastly across a plain toward some distant mountains."

"YOU!" Clara hollered, her black eyes flashing with a mosaic of emotion. Then her voice faltered. The feelings were simply too elaborate for her to express in words. Clara's face at that moment was a gem, cut with compassion—an ever changing prism of vulnerability.

"You good woman, Dee ah NAH!" she blurted out, using an index finger to hammer the point home.

"Thanks, Clara," I replied, honoured.

A slim paring of a moon wafted in and out of sight in the south while South Mountain stood, a holy shrine.

What happened the day that Clara and I sat on the hill was a special merging of windblown pine, squirrel chatter, sisterspirit, and dreaming mountains. We sat together swaying in the arms of the cosmic mother. We shared the silence, as only true friends can do. Time was marked by the soaring of the raven above the tall black spires. And even though for me, time had taken on a scent of urgency, I suddenly realized that I had let go. I had let go of my dream of an ideal female neighbour. Clara's very presence emanated support. The friendship that had begun so far off base had gradually become profound in its own form. Even though the literary connection could never exist between us, with a flash I realized we were doing the one thing I had originally believed impossible. After all, what had spiralled out of the silence but a sharing of stories?

# *Clara and Death*

S omewhere off in the darkness a large tree cracked and plunged
to earth. Natty Creek thundered by, its chocolate-hued waters
hurling themselves over both spillways and keeping us all on
our toes in case the dam should burst. Jay had accepted a job as assistant surveyor on the Iskut Road, and even though he slaved away
at home on his days off, the bulk of the huge autumn harvest had
shifted to my shoulders. Certainly we could put to good use the two
hundred dollars he earned each day. But I was twisted inside by the
thought of him assisting in the demise of the wilderness. Downstream
on the Ningunsaw River, the pile driver had begun work and the
head-banging crash sounded out the death knell with stunning regularity. The steel pipes they were hammering into the riverbed were
more than thirty feet long. They were, in effect, crucifying the
Ningunsaw.

Jay was so caught up in the excitement of a rare job away from
home and new contacts that much of the time he scarcely noticed
what I was doing. Somehow I managed to scribble between chores.
Apart from the regular tasks was a myriad of harvest jobs. There were
poppies to pull, grain to cut, root crops to dig, and parsley, celery,

oregano, and basil to reap and dry. How sobering it was to realize that it would take the kids and I fifteen days simply to bring in the carrots, which would amount to nearly a thousand pounds.

It had been an unusually wet summer and fall, and large puddles resided between the rows. Normally we didn't wash carrots at all, but this season the soil clung to them in clumps. If left to my own devices, I would have washed them right away by swishing them in buckets from the shallow creek. Jay insisted that I simply pull them and leave them lying. "Let the rain wash them," he advised.

"What if it freezes?" I asked. After all it was September. He shot me a dirty look and replied, "We can protect them with floating row cover. Besides, a little frost won't hurt them."

The following day Nat and Ben pitched in, starting where I had finished the previous afternoon. Toiling steadily and twisting the tops off as we went along, we worked our way down half of the three-hundred-foot row. The discarded tops provided a mattress along which we lined the tubers. The brilliant day would inevitably be followed by a hard frost.

In the evening Jay charged down the hill as if his pants were on fire. Bursting through the back door he hollered, "Nat and Ben will have to do the dishes tonight because Mom and I have a lot of work to do!" The smell of roast rabbit wafted through the room, but the delicious dinner was ruined by the tension in the air. Worn out already, I was in no shape to pick up a 150-foot row of carrots, which had been planted triple in places.

Still, stoically I grabbed buckets and scrambled down the hill after Jay. In the failing light we gathered the glowing orange roots. We then lugged the twelve bulging five-gallon buckets to the wheelhouse for the night, to protect them from impending frost.

The next morning I found a note on the windowsill that read, "Clean and sort carrots in wheelhouse." I felt a surge of anger. What I had wanted to do was to pull only as many carrots as I could have comfortably cleaned and put away. And what would have happened if I had simply followed my own inclinations? In so many instances with Jay I felt damned if I did and damned if I didn't.

Gradually I realized I felt inadequate around him because somewhere deep within my psyche I felt that Jay was right about me. If anything, he nurtured my own lack of self-esteem. For many years I felt if only I could do better, do more, be more. If only I could be someone other than myself. Yet at a deeper level a voice cried out for love. And was denied.

The whole struggle left me in a state of confusion, where the main priority had become, quite simply, my own survival. The temperature had plunged to below freezing. And overnight the soil had hardened, making the cleaning miserable work. Our hands ached, as for hours Nat and I scrubbed carrots in icy water. At last, with black and broken fingernails and palms prickling with pain, we toiled up to the root cellar with the fifty-pound pails.

Reaching the yard with relief I rested briefly by my new flower bed. I thought of spring, when the blush of blue forget-me-nots had been intercepted by the shout of calendulas, and the amaranth dangled bright pink tassels. Remembering, more recently, the jet of Copenhagen that had been shot onto one of the rocks surrounding the bed, I pictured Clara and wondered what she was doing these shrinking autumn days.

I could imagine her bustling about her small house, getting lost in the tangles of twine she undid and wound up neatly, in the piecing together of her well-worn puzzle. I imagined her weathered face adopting the serene lustre that came with feeling safe and at peace. She didn't (couldn't) write lists the way I did, didn't jot down too many goals to fit into a day, didn't frustrate herself in a frantic race against the descending darkness. Surely her eyes glinted as she pat-a-caked her bread into form, her diminutive dark head dreaming back to when she was a young girl beside the Stikine River.

Clara didn't primp, even though she spruced up for Sundays. I wondered if she ever looked in a mirror. And what she saw. I could see her at the sink diligently scrubbing away at the weary soup pot. And she was content with her work even if it left behind scabs of moose soup.

On our weekly visits I longed to compare notes about our times apart. How had her week been? What had she been thinking about? How was it going with the "old man"? Her inevitable reply, delivered with optimism, was "Good." Yet it couldn't have all been good because I saw the storms pass through, had witnessed random black glowers. Did she simply say this as part of the meeting ceremony? Or was she an enlightened one, who didn't succumb to petty annoyances, the blight of the lives of so many so-called normal women?

In my imagination I rose above Natty Creek and the Ningunsaw Valley and saw myself bustling about my log mansion, ever tense lest I displease the "god" with whom I lived. In a more modest abode high up the hill to the east I saw Clara rummaging, ruminating, taking an hour to cut a carrot if she felt like it. I marvelled at her life, which was so simple beside mine. But then was it? With her weak mental capacity, maybe every manoeuvre in the waking world was a chore for her. Granted, I saw over and over that glint in her eye, saw the face of the wise old woman rise to the surface, then vanish again like it had never been there. Who truly knew with Clara? I flashed on the endless cycle of chores that so many of us, as women, were locked into. The invisible work. I accomplished far more than Clara but wasn't most of it, in the end, invisible? It occurred to me that ultimately she may be the smart one.

The rain continued and Jay was let off work for several days. He took the kids and I to town in the Bronco he had been loaned by the mining company. We left home in the driving rain without the faintest glint of morning light. Ben sobbed as we stumbled up the steep hill.

At Bell 11, the truck stop thirty miles south, Jay gave us five minutes to eat breakfast because he was worried about our dam. It was the first time we had been to town as a family in two years, yet I felt like we were on our way home before we had even arrived in Stewart. As we rattled along, the road was pocked with overflowing potholes. The earth was saturated and new streams virtually leaped out of the hillsides. Fresh waterfalls cascaded over the banks and filled the ditches with murkiness. The Bell Irving River strained to break free of its bed.

Between Meziadin Junction and Stewart I felt like I was drowning. It was as though the mountainsides had sprung leaks and where one would never imagine a stream, a torrent now flung itself toward the valley bottom. On one steep face, where there were usually three waterfalls visible, Natalia counted twenty-two.

We rumbled across the bridge above a teeming Bear River and had only stepped into the Stewart post office when the lights went out. Most of the town was left in darkness. I managed to mail an envelope to Peter Burford just before an apologetic postmistress dashed off to deal with an overflowing toilet. Water, water, was everywhere. We had only two hours to poke through the darkened stores and buy our supplies. At the King Edward Hotel, cold sandwiches and cold drinks were all that were available, and after an uninspiring lunch, we headed back to the Ningunsaw Valley. We were all relieved to find the dam secure.

Weatherwise, what a contrast was in store for us when, in the same month, we had the chance to fly with Jay and his boss to Eskay Creek. It was the scene of what was said to be the richest gold find in North America and was also the destination of the Iskut Road. The sky was completely clear during the twenty-minute flight, which took us twenty-five miles south to the mine. It lay halfway between our homestead and the border of the Alaska Panhandle. A sea of jagged Coast Mountain peaks, adorned with new snow, flowed, wave after wave, toward the Pacific Ocean. However, as we approached Eskay

Creek I saw an elaborate and ugly network of roads scarring the mountainside. As yet there was air access only, and all machinery and supplies had been flown in. Flying freight was costly business and many far-flung camps, such as this, found it more economical, when they pulled out, to leave the goods behind.

At four thousand feet the terrain was mossy with stunted balsams. The camp was a cluster of small, blue-plywood shacks connected by boardwalks, now coated with a fine layer of fresh snow. It faced a high, gold-coloured cliff that caught the sun in a startling way as we left the chopper. The original squat log cabin, built in the early 1900s by Tom MacKay, the first white man to arrive there, still stood at the mine site.

While Jay attended to some business in an office, the children and I approached the cookhouse. Outside hung a dry, faded Christmas wreath from the previous year. We shyly entered a stark room lined with long tables. Windows were scant. But in plain view through the kitchen door was the cook. With huge eyes Ben stared at the man in the white uniform and towering chef's hat, with blanched hair and beard, and skin the colour of pink lemonade. Hundreds of miles from civilization, such formal dress looked bizarre. The chef was in the process of preparing a goliath turkey for roasting. His assistant, in checkerboard pants, with black wavy hair and able biceps, welcomed us, offering soft drinks, juice, or coffee. This progressed to French fries, which Nat and Ben eagerly accepted. I rarely made them and they were a town treat. When I told the man we were his closest neighbours, the Ningunsaw Valley meant nothing to him. He was from Vancouver. It felt like a strange dream to enter this scene so far off in the mountains.

On the way back we whirled above Volcano Creek, the planned route for the Iskut Road, then veered east and followed the Iskut River home. From above, the broad expanse of river flat was ochre islands of sand and leafless trees, braided together by surging manes of mighty green water. Although I did my best to fasten my attention on the river, my eyes were tugged toward a mammoth piece of equipment chewing away at the earth.

Far below a cow moose and her calf, royal in their winter wear, raced across the road and ducked into a willow thicket. Meanwhile, hideous-looking machines called belly scrapers scooped up river gravel, then bounded at astonishing speed, past the creatures' frail shelter. The road itself was a single strip of destruction. What followed would be far worse. The devastation of clear-cut logging and mining would alter the land I loved in drastic ways.

As a bald eagle soared toward an ivory peak west of the river, I remembered that above all humanity needed to undergo a spiritual transformation, an awakening that left all vitally aware that we are one with the spruce, wolf, moose, mountain—the very air. How could anyone thoughtlessly destroy it then?

When we glided back to our valley, Nat spotted Julie from the chopper window. Then I saw her, running like someone possessed, down the trail toward our clearing. Her hat flew off and she stopped to retrieve it. Later we learned that Gilbert, who was already at our place, had refused to wait for her. Clara hadn't come, and back at the Handel home the soup must have been boiling furiously, ready for when her children returned. In my own house the loft above the wood cookstove was crammed with the green tomatoes I had picked and packed up from the garden.

The next day, birch and poplar trees quivered in the wind, releasing their rain of golden leaves as I attached twine to the roots of solid heads of cabbage. Then with six dangling from each hand, I trudged past the pond and up the hill to the root cellar.

Later in the gusty afternoon beneath an indigo sky, with hens scratching at our feet, Nat, Ben, and I gathered rosehips in the yard. As I plucked the festive baubles I thought of Clara, who had helped me with this task the weekend prior. We were women in what was still, predominantly, a man's world. Most of our visitors were male and some of them were rifle-toting, wolf-hating, grade A machos. It was still the way of the north. We felt the presence of our own breasts, our smallness and vulnerability beside the big chests and bravado. Completely out of touch with the feminine in their natures, they failed to round themselves out. Clara and I tried to bring to light our masculine selves, the animus, which was released in shouts from her and iron persistence from me. I knew what I needed to do and I had stayed on the writing path despite the fierce resistance.

*Mother Earth News* had prominently featured the reprint of my story "Living the Dream." In addition, they had asked for more and had responded positively to my suggestion of an article about huckleberries. Fan letters continued to trickle in from all over the United States. Further, a request for a feature gardening story from Liz Primeau, editor of *Canadian Gardening,* gave me more confidence to proceed. Yet what shone the brightest was the book contract I had signed with Lyons and Burford in New York. I had received it in December 1991. Each morning throughout the winter and now in the spring of 1992 I would stuff pads of paper, pens, dictionary, thesaurus, old journals, and a thermos of creamy coffee into my pack and tensely trek down to the German cabin to write.

The little log house was frigid this particular morning and despite the five-minute amble through the trees, I knew the blood would soon slow in my veins. I exhaled small white ghosts into the deathly still room. The smell of balsam wood chips drifted up to my nostrils as I hastily built a fire in the dwarf heater. The flames crackled in appreciation of my offering. To combat the cold I wore boots with felt liners, long johns, wool pants, a heavy wool sweater and a thick Icelandic toque.

I spread my work in front of me on the rough hand-hewn table into which the Germans had carved their names alongside the names of their sweethearts. To make it cosier I had hung blue curtains. Beyond the window, the clearing was surrounded by two-hundred-foot emerald spruce trees. Beneath each was a branchy haven for creatures in the storms of winter, and at the tiptop, lookout posts. One now swayed with the song of a grosbeak. But my underlying feeling was one of fear because I knew my action was going against the grain of my husband's need to control. Equally as strong was my own need to express myself in words. Each day I scribbled for four hours. My solitude was intercepted by occasional visits from Natalia and Ben. But this morning my pen was halted by the arrival of a wolf.

I felt his wild presence at my left shoulder. Glancing out the window I caught the black ruff and cool approach. If the glass hadn't been there, from where I sat I could have easily reached out and touched him. The predominantly black coat was flecked with lighter-hued hair. What struck me most were the untamed golden eyes. The long sinewy legs and large feet that had roamed the Stikine watershed year after year paced their electric way past the cabin. As the wolf glided by I caught the scent of fear, but was it in me? Intelligence and primal knowing resonated in his dark form.

Leaping up, I crept over to the wooden door with its small pane of glass. Impulsively I grabbed the lever handle and pulled it tight toward me. And as I gazed, with racing heart and avid curiosity, the creature caught my eye. His ebony ears pricked up as he raised his hefty yet tapered jaw. After a probing, golden-eyed stare, which struck a wild chord in me, he loped off down the trail, following Natty Creek toward Willow Park. I stared after his shimmering form.

Minutes later I opened the door and descended the rough plank steps. What I saw when I glanced north made me jump. No more than twenty feet away the wolf stood staring at me. As minute hairs prickled along my spine, I realized the creature had doubled back and come through the timber flanking the base of the hill. Once again we stood face to face. He stared at me with uncanny familiarity.

Regrettably, the wolf's boldness was intensified by hunger. This became apparent when he crept into our clearing one night and attacked Gandhi, our prize gander who had so often bitten Clara. The next night Gandhi's favourite hen, Dub Dub, was killed and a gravely wounded Gandhi was finished off. Abruptly a brood of seven three-day-old goslings was orphaned. As much as I had resisted the idea, it became clear to us that the wolf had to go. It was simply too daring and would continue to stalk our domestic animals. The bodies of the two geese, which the wolf had had no chance to eat, were found and Jay set traps in the garden, marked by goose wings.

Three days later the marauding wolf was caught. Its dark hide blended with the soil and it was almost too painful to watch as, like a squirming piece of earth, it cowered toward the raspberry bushes, dragging its snarl of traps.

The morning Jay shot the wolf happened to be a Sunday. The body was still lying in front of the greenhouse when Clara came onto the clearing. It was most unusual for her to arrive first and alone. She was clearly proud of herself. Jay, the children, and I were in the garden when we heard the doors slam explosively from forty feet up the hill. Clara had many ways of getting attention.

"We're down here," Nat and I hollered from our squat positions in the asparagus patch. As she proceeded down the path to the pond, my friend looked nearly formal in a crisp cowboy shirt and carefully chosen jeans. Bursting out of the leafy tunnel, with a mission in mind and a ponytail ready to break loose of its elastic, Clara lunged toward me. Her wiry hand extended, she took my own and pumped it vigorously.

"Tank oo bery much, Dee ah NAH! Tank oo bery much for kil ling dat wofe."

"It wasn't me. Jay shot the wolf," I said, suppressing my laughter. At this news she regarded me with a deadpan gaze, then lumbered over to Jay, where she repeated the ceremony. Jay responded with a cock-eyed grin.

Later, when the rest of the Handel family arrived, we buried the poor creature and at my request stood around his grave in a circle while I said a prayer. I hated to see any wild animal die at the hands of humans, and even after so many years still grieved for the moose who fell to sustain us.

But Clara didn't hold any great love for wolves, and when she had caught wind of this one roaming our clearing right to the back door step, she had waited for it to materialize in their front yard, or worse, somewhere on the trail. Clara avoided danger zones and vibrated like a grouse feather in the breeze if a bear emerged from the emerald foliage or a wolf crept past on padded paws, its bristle illuminated in the starlight.

Clara also possessed an elemental fear of death. And she dealt with death by sitting for long spells with a plug of tobacco in her cheek and a giant tin cup of either vinegar water or near-lethal black tea in front of her, mulling over the disappearance of loved ones from her life. Clara cared deeply for others, and it was painful for her to watch people vanish from her earth walk.

What I remember about the death of Clara's brother, Morris, was how burdened she was by it, weighed down by more than her day pack and heavy jaw, as she twisted the burl knob and stepped into the entryway of our house. A few days earlier the Handels had been up to the funeral in Iskut, and the event lingered in Clara's mind. She tried to make sense of it by repeating the reality to herself like a mantra. Once Fritz had ducked his way into our kitchen and perched himself, with a thoughtful expression, on the step, his wife asked him repeatedly: "Why Mor ris die, Fitz?" Fritz rested his elbows on his knees and repeated his reply with the patience of a priest.

"I don't know, Clara. I guess he just got so sick he died."

With eyebrows pursed, Clara pondered his words, her mouth sagging more with each passing moment. On the counter, a batch of bread made from our own wheat radiated nutty richness. Jay had recently shot a moose, and in the warming oven was a plate stacked high with paper-thin pieces of breaded moose liver.

After we had all feasted on this favoured dish, I invited Clara on a walk to the site of the moose kill. The path angled west through a tall vibrant forest skirting the river flat. As we proceeded, she spoke of Morris, conjuring up his presence and his passing.

"Why Mor ris die, Dee Ah NAH?"

I felt a weight bear down on my breast because when Clara asked me a question I felt obliged to answer. And one thing was certain. I didn't have all the answers. However, I knew she heard me when I said, "I'm so sorry about your brother, Clara." Her shoulders, clad in multiple layers, dropped slightly. I could smell the drift of Copenhagen from her mouth.

Even when we arrived at the kill site, with its crater of trampled snow, smeared here and there with patches of faded blood and clumps of moose hair, my friend's mind dwelled on the death of her brother.

"Morris isn't suffering anymore, Clara.... And you know, sometimes things happen for reasons hidden from human knowing." Her small, spry form seemed to gain strength from my words, and when our eyes met I felt a communication deep in my soul. The Ningunsaw River tumbled jade green and the peaks on the far side glowed with hope. It was a mild day and cottonwood buds were swelling while snow collapsed beneath a gathering of scrubby balsam.

We had viewed the site of the sacrifice and there seemed no reason to linger there. Daily life was tugging on my sleeve. I wanted to serve baked potatoes with moose roast for supper, and I needed to get the spuds in the oven. I said as much to Clara, and as I turned she did too, like my own shadow. My snowboots formed a warm cocoon around each foot as I retraced our route. Jay had spanned a former river channel by cutting alder poles and lining it with them. I crossed the wobbly bridge first, then waited for Clara to follow. With face clenched, she willed her too-large boots to float her across.

On the far side of the hollow, a whisky jack released a rusty peep into the sky and Clara asked me for the hundredth time, "Why Morris die?"

Spinning around I was struck by her misery. I reached out. Just before encompassing her in a tight compassionate hug, I caught the quicksilver change of mood in her pebble eyes. Despite the solemnity of the occasion, at the prospect of affection, Clara's expression had changed from one of despair to one of near devilish delight.

# *The Last Summer*

The last summer I saw Clara my life was in turmoil. My world was spinning in mad circles and I was hanging on in desperation, battling the momentum that threatened to shatter me along with the dream I had been living for thirteen years. Such a brilliant July, and yet it only seemed to make a mockery of my misery. I longed to reach up to the sun, as I had done with the lamps as the children drifted into sleep, and lower the light that only accentuated the cracks of a crumbling existence.

Clara's face was more creased than ever the last time I saw her. She understood my need to leave. She had seen it coming. But mostly she saw the disappearance of her best friend. And when I looked at her weathered face I felt fresh grief well up in me.

At the end of June, Jay had taken both children on a six-week vacation to Wisconsin to visit his mother, two sisters, and twelve brothers. Under normal circumstances I would have revelled in this rare alone time and poured myself into the completion of my book. However, a letter he had given me the day before leaving had hurled me into a state of shock.

For so long, through bouts of outrageous behaviour that would have sent most women packing, I had staunchly maintained that we could work things out. I desperately wanted my marriage to move through the necessary changes, and to continue. After all, the stakes were monumental. My family life, my home, and my beloved valley in which I had become deeply rooted, were all part of what I stood to lose. And I would be forced back into civilization, which had become not only alien but also objectionable. Despite the profound losses, I couldn't turn away from the truth. For the sake of my own survival, I had no choice but to leave. At least for now.

The memory of an incident, which had occurred the day before Jay and the kids departed, will stay with me forever. Some friends from one hundred miles north in Glenora—Lynne Thunderstorm and two of her children, Fox and Raven—had paid an overnight visit. We didn't see them often, but they led a similar lifestyle and Lynne and I exchanged letters. She knew our marriage was in trouble, and that night we sat up with Jay while she tried, with all her verbal dexterity, to reach him. Lynne had been fluent and calm while Jay had grown more hostile. The next morning Jay had presented me with a letter. He thought that he was capable of making the best decisions for all of us. His letter stated, in essence, that unless I granted him all of the decision-making power in our lives, he didn't wish to be married to me anymore.

A little later, much against Jay's wishes, Natalia, Ben, and I walked our company up the hill and across the clear-cut to where their truck was parked. It was all I could do to keep myself from simply walking away. Lynne felt we should leave. Instead, after seeing them off, we started home. Ben cried frequently. Long-legged Nat, who had charged ahead, was soon out of sight, her form swallowed by the forest. As Ben and I descended the steep slope into the woods, I was brought to an abrupt halt by the strangest sound. Was it roosters crowing? Over and over the crazy cry echoed up and down the mountainside. My spine tingled as I suddenly realized that the voice was screaming,

"Ben! Ben! Ben!" and that it was Jay. He sounded as if he had an arrow stuck in his back. I clutched Ben. It struck me that I may have made the worst mistake of my life by returning at all. "Don't answer!" I hissed, then tentatively called back to Jay myself. We caught sight of the red beret as he approached through the forest. I called out, "Have you seen Nat?"

"No." He answered from only a few feet away. He looked bewildered and his eyes were darting frantically from side to side. "I haven't seen Nat, but we'd better start looking for her because this is bear season. She might be ripped apart already!" He shouted her name. For an endless moment, I was locked into a state of absolute terror, wondering whether my daughter was safe or maimed.

Abruptly Jay stopped calling and turned toward me. His face was waxen with fury. He admitted that he had met Natalia on the trail and that she was already down at the house. He just wanted me to know what it felt like all the times when Nat and I took off during bear season and didn't even say where we were going. My mind reeled. I was fully aware that Natalia had dashed away before I'd had a chance to tell her to stay with us. As Jay came closer, I felt that it was futile to attempt to defend my position. In fact, I felt almost frozen. While his hands vibrated in front of me, I stayed as still as a statue. Not a single word emerged from my mouth. Then like lightning Jay's mood changed. He scooped up Ben, settled him on his shoulders, and trotted down the trail, babbling about all of the relatives Ben would meet in Wisconsin and the fun they would have. Slowly the terror loosened its grip on my body. What was left was the ashes of my dream. I felt singed by the fire of his breath, and by what I had read in his gaze. At that moment I felt no desire to ever look into his eyes again.

Indifferent to my despair, the valley went through its rebirth. White flower season slowly transformed to pink and mauve. First the wild roses flared along the slope to the pond, their deep fuschia petals bowing in the restless coastal breeze. Next the fireweed unfurled. In agony I gyrated around the grieving circle. It was a saving grace that there was enough to do to keep me grounded.

One morning I awoke alone, as usual, and stared out the window at the snow patches on South Mountain, unaware that today I would learn how the downfall of our homestead would have a ripple effect.

On the front porch, I cut the twine and cracked open bundles of homegrown wheat for the chickens and geese. Next, with Spooky at my heels, I wandered toward the river gathering horsetails for the geese. Attached to the belt of my green cotton pants was a sheath containing a can of bear spray, in case I encountered an ornery visitor.

Once the geese were gulping down the coarse wild fodder, I trotted down the hill to gather clover for the rabbits. Since they were now housed in the new barn, it took more effort to feed them. First I hauled the stuffed buckets up a ladder balanced against the outside of the barn. My load was featherweight compared to the grief I carried inside. Once past the beehives, the final obstacle was a hay mound, over which I crawled to get to the cages. Dividing the greens between the sceptical bucks and moody does, I then scrambled back down the ladder. Grabbing goose and chicken buckets, I poured the dregs on my flower bed, scampered down the hill to the pond where I scrubbed the pails with horsetails, then filled and packed them back up to the barn.

After a fried egg breakfast, I felt sunlight flood the clearing and, rushing down to the garden, I flung open the door of the greenhouse. Touring, I shook all of the blossoming tomatoes. Next, I needed to pump water up to the house. Negotiating a log straddling the creek, I cursed as I yanked, without effect, on the cord of the gasoline pump. At last it caught and I dashed up the slope, hoping the hose would stay in one of the water barrels, which were located inside the house.

Clambering across the canning shelves, necessary to scale in order to reach the three barrels located on top of the highest shelf, I knocked a glass sealer down. It smashed. Spooky dashed and hid.

Once the containers were full, I scurried back down the hill and turned the pump off by shorting it out with a screwdriver.

Minutes later I was back in the house grinding wheat to make bread. Due to the long summer days, I could leave my three daily hours of garden work until later. It was all routine and for brief moments I lost myself in it, forgetting that this self-sufficient rhythm would be coming to an abrupt end.

Each day I also tried to spend four hours working on my book. I finally had it spread out in front of me on the pine table when Spooky's bark announced the arrival of the Handels.

The four of them trooped into the kitchen looking awkward, yet authentic in their sorrow. Clara stood astride, resembling a small and sullen prize fighter. One eye was black.

"What happened to your eye, Clara?" I blurted out. Before Clara could tussle the words out, Gilbert piped up.

"She was trying to pack too much up the hill at once and she got so frustrated she punched herself in the eye."

"It's embarrassing," Fritz added, lest anyone think he was the source of the shiner.

"What was she packing up the hill?" I said, sensing tension in the air.

"Her stuff," Julie volunteered.

"We're leaving," Fritz stated, then meeting my eyes he added, "We're doing this in support of you." His face was drawn and serious. Approaching the table, he held out a gift of Philadelphia cream cheese from the Iskut Co-op in his work-worn hand. Then Gilbert stepped forward, his green eyes glittering with sympathy, and handed me some candies from deep in his pocket.

It soon came to light that the Handel family was in the process of moving back to the place near Kinaskan Lake, where they had lived when Julie and Gilbert were babies. The move would be gradual. They had many belongings to haul. But by the time I had departed the Ningunsaw Valley, they would be gone as well.

Fritz sank to the step that separated the kitchen from the main living area.

"Jay made the mistake of his life giving you that letter," he said. From his pocket he drew one he was leaving for Jay and handed it to me. I read the neat script. "I am greatly saddened by the fact that you could leave your wife such a letter. You owe much to Deanna, as do Clara and my kids. The place would not be the same if Deanna and the kids were to leave."

I was astonished and deeply moved by this strong show of support. The Handels were sacrificing a cosy home that had been the result of two years of intensive labour. Thanks to Jay I had come to believe my presence in the valley held little significance. Their stand clearly told me how important I was to them.

In the letter Fritz went on to say that he found Jay locked into an ideology that didn't allow him to admit any weakness or error, and that philosophically they were 180 degrees apart. While Jay's personality type adhered to the law of the jungle, Fritz was an advocate of co-operation. And even though he had cast off Darwin's theory of evolution twenty years earlier, Fritz still had to resist the pull of such dogma. Significantly, through his struggle he had regained empathy and compassion. In his letter he once again emphasized, "Darwinism brought to its logical conclusion produced the Holocaust."

I invited the Handels for dinner and they accepted. Julie came to the garden with me and we gathered potatoes, carrots, salad fixings, beets, and onions. We also prepared two jars labelled "Fritz's leg," from a hindquarter of moose Fritz had given us.

An hour later the five of us soberly savoured the prime food set out on the table, but there was no feeling of festivity. Clara ate her supper with a vacant stare. After dinner, Fritz, true to form, washed the dishes. There was a finality contained in his movements. We had shared so many Sundays. But we all knew that what had become a comfortable routine was at an end. Our whole lives, in fact, were being blown apart to reassemble in far-flung places.

I offered them a dozen brown eggs for the last time, and Fritz stepped into the entryway as I was retrieving them from the windowsill.

"Well, then, this is good-bye," he said and gave me a warm hug. Julie and Gilbert filed by, their gumboots stomping reluctantly down the steps. Each in turn grasped me lightly. Clara was last. With elbows akimbo and a look of eternal sorrow on her small brown face, she threw her arms around my neck and hugged me hard.

"Doan wor ree, Dee ah NAH! Doan wor ree!"

The family departed back down the trail and once again I was left alone. Somehow, though, I knew I would see Clara again.

With grace, the routine encompassed me and served as a shield against what I had to cope with. And it was a blessing that my soul was, more than once, stirred by surprise.

One day, as I walked by the pond, I saw a female merganser and seven freshly hatched babies swimming across it. No matter which way the mother darted, the babies were right behind. The tiny two-toned balls of fluff moved as if they were connected by invisible strings. The mother, spotting me, led her brood to the far spillway, where they seemed to vanish into the tumble of rock and water. Intrigued, I peered under the boards to see if they were hiding in a corner, then strolled along, sceptically scanning the second waterway. Later I was to read that mergansers are agile in water right from birth and are known for their amazing vanishing acts.

Another day, as I lay on my stomach by the pond cleaning off the intake screen with a hoe I unexpectedly scooped a toad from the wire mesh. Repulsed, I stared at his bloated body and protruding tongue. Clearly the creature was dead. Gently, I laid him on his back to my right, then continued work on my belly, scraping off the debris. When I glanced over again, to my amazement, the toad had flipped over and was lying there watching me. An hour later, he had limped away with one damaged front leg. Like the mergansers, he had vanished from my view and had gotten on with his life.

Small marvels continued to nudge me onward. From friends out for a visit I learned about a destitute pilgrim named George Walter who was walking through the mountain passes, following the Stewart-Cassiar Highway. He had a trailing beard, wore an ankle-length patch-work denim robe, and carried a modest crosspiece. On his head rode a modified cowboy hat, while on his feet he simply wore sandals. George Walter had been walking for twenty years on his own private crusade. Biking back from Bob Quinn Lake one day I spotted sandal tracks along the edge of the lonely road and knew that George had wandered through, his mysteries intact. Thinking about him, I remembered Clara's long journey on foot and realized that she also contained the mysterious as well as the divine.

The annual blizzard of cottonwood fluff swirled around me as I hoed horsetails and hilled the potatoes. Frequently I reminded my-self that even as I toiled in the vegetable patch, I was also letting go. It was heart-wrenching to realize that for the first fall in thirteen years, the children and I wouldn't be feasting on our produce. Even so, on a sunny day, the garden was where I wanted to be.

Crouching beside a two-hundred-foot row of beets, I glanced up and saw Clara bounding toward me, her obsidian eyes twinkling. She had come to help and was soon kneeling beside me. With the bless-ing of the sun on our backs we squatted our way along, while Clara asked, "Dis wan, Dee ah NAH? Dis wan?" pointing to each weed be-fore daring to pluck it.

Beyond the garden and toward the towering woods, the giant umbrellas of cow parsnip floated above a sea of green created by tall grass, stinging nettles, wild raspberry, and elderberry, all embracing the fallen fir giants.

For me weeding was largely a meditative act. I preferred to sink into the soil and wordlessly work around the fledgling beets, weeding and thinning them and cleansing my mind at the same time. It was tiresome monitoring Clara's every move, but I flashed back to the beginning and realized how far she had come.

That first spring, when Fritz had taken prime potatoes and stuck them in the ground, Clara could only stand and shake her head, absolutely unable to grasp why her intelligent husband would choose to bury perfectly good food.

Now beneath the blazing summer sun, while the hummingbird moths landed on the lilies and the pungent smell of cow parsnips drifted across the yard, while the mosquito bit vindictively and the kingfisher cried, Clara crouched by my side. She now saw the sense of gardening. Yes. She saw even more.

Glancing up, Clara motioned toward the turban of a bright yellow lily in the next row.

"Dat pre tee, Dee ah NAH!" A mild shock passed through my body. Stunned, I nodded in agreement. This was the same woman who, initially, hadn't appeared to see the beauty around her. Yet for me, it had meant so much to live amidst the splendour of the north that I had endured a sometimes tortuous relationship simply to stay there.

With her fine fingers burrowing into the earth, Clara helped me weed. Reaching deep beneath the tap roots, she lifted the nettles and cottonwood seedlings. At the same time she helped me to hoist my own roots out of the valley. Mindfully she dislodged the fine root hairs that had become so intimately linked with the soil. But no matter how careful she was, some were torn away and stayed behind. In the same sense, pieces of my own roots were being ripped away and would remain in the soil that had sustained me for so long.

Clara worked her shaman magic unaware, helping me through the gut-slicing process of leaving. Her dark head bowed to the earth and the serious angle of her jaw matched the tone of the soil. With silent rhythm she followed, yet gave me enough space to experience the separateness that was now flooding in from all directions. In the long months together our sisterspirit had merged, and like the twin I had left so long ago, I had learned to flow with and accept my shadow self.

As her dainty fingers dug into the earth, Clara helped to lift me out of my despair, to see that there was still a self separate from all I had become. And that all I had become would go with me now.

The temperature was rising, and beads of sweat dotted Clara's brow. Even though she wore cut-off shorts, she motioned toward my tank top, which was her way of asking if I had another one. Since I didn't, I suggested she simply wear her bra.

"It's just girls here," I reasoned. For the rest of the afternoon Clara proudly pranced around in her padded bra, likely found at the dump. Frequently she pointed out the diagonal scar below her ribcage from her gall bladder operation.

We dipped in the frigid pond together. My pal couldn't swim, but she showed a surge of pride after daring to plunge into the viciously cold water. Then, after flicking the dried goose droppings into the waterfall, Clara daintily spread a towel on the boards spanning the spillway and sat down.

Unexpectedly, and with fresh appreciation, I saw a certain beauty in Clara as she soaked up the sun. Her face was serene, the afternoon light caught and held the shelf of a prominent cheekbone, and her coarse ebony hair gleamed from the dunking. In this oblique moment I caught the flash of beauty in the black eyes that held the ancient stories of her ancestors, caught and held them there, never to be released through the all-too-intricate dance of the tongue.

At the same time that we basked in the radiant sunshine, my heart was breaking into tiny pieces. My friend felt it too and shared my pain.

Twice Clara and I had been through the cycles of the seasons together, had felt the tug of the moon twenty-six times. For two years we had shared nearly every Sunday, had become close in a way I hadn't thought possible in the beginning. Now the death of all this stalked us, darting in and out of the trees along the shadowy eastern ridge, casting handfuls of darkness down upon us even as we revelled in the rebirth of summer.

The days were endless and there was no need for Clara to rush away. It was my custom in the evening to perch on the front porch and drink in the peace and beauty of my surroundings. I invited Clara to sit with me and she nodded gravely. Pulling on sweaters, we sat close together on the rickety blue bench and watched the evening drift by. Around the corner a hen was having a fit—a late egg layer. A green wind spun the tiny poplar leaves on the hillside while a kitten named Ricki Ticki wound his tail around Spooky and ambled perilously close to the edge of the unrailed porch. The slopes and flat blushed magenta with fireweed. Below, lily goblets gleamed in the garden. Again and again my eyes scanned the lush clearing, then followed the restless ridge of the western peaks. Above, an empty sky was lidded by a melting silver cloud. I sat enduring the pain, knowing that some would remain in me forever.

Clara's face was clenched against her fate. Her people had known the need to depart again and again, even though their hair and eyes had grown attached to the terrain. Nomadic by nature, they had moved with rhythmic regularity. She knew about the river of life that carried us all along. Yet, day after day, she had watched her own husband toil as he burrowed into the hillside to dig out an earth home for his family.

With me, she had found a friendship like no other. Clara could have happily spent the rest of her days walking "leetle" walks with me, tramping down from her house on the hill to spend a festive Sunday. She could have turned her woman circles, meshing her movements with mine, delighting in the flow and also my acceptance of who she was. Like the puzzles over which Clara laboured, all of the pieces of her life had fallen into place. She longed to battle the current and stay. So did I.

By the last summer my tolerance had evolved to the level of deep appreciation. I had come to realize that as we learn to embrace others, including their ugly parts, we also learn to accept the harder-to-love parts of ourselves. And the more we search for and see the nobility in another soul, the brighter our own light shines.

The Ningunsaw Valley was the only place I truly wanted to be. As I gazed out over it I could not contain the torrent of emotion swelling up in me.

The last time I saw Clara she was so silent, but when a wail burst from my throat, she joined me. Our cries rang out across the towering trees, to echo in the ancient icefields. Down the windswept Iskut Canyon the wolves pricked up their ears. Then they howled with us.

ℴℯℴℯℴℯℴ

# *Epilogue*

I t has been more than four years since I last saw Clara, but somehow her spirit has remained with me. Fritz and I continue to
correspond across the thousand miles that now lie between our
two families. Ever adaptable, Fritz rebuilt and has sent pictures of
Clara settled into her new home. Communication with my buddy has
been scant and usually comes through Julie in the form of, "Clara says
hi," or "Clara misses you."

Being a person who forms strong connections to place, I returned
with my children to Shuswap Lake. Here the root system is substantial. Sooner or later we have all returned. After thirteen years in the
wilderness, and such a profound loss, I needed the love and support
of family.

Quietly Natalia, Ben, and I weathered the stress of culture shock,
coupled with the chasm of our grief. Initially the noise and speed of
this strange civilization were almost unbearable. Still, it has been great
to be able to share small moments with my family again. Part of my
reason for returning was to give my own children the opportunity
to know their relatives, whose visits north were so vital, yet so fleeting.

What about new friendships with women? When I first arrived, and was still in my rawest stage of grieving and struggling to adjust to what had become an alien culture, I met Joy. She lived across the road and was a porcelain doll artist, painter, mother, and grandmother. Aptly named, her wisdom often helped me to see the light at the end of the tunnel. Joy has been something of a guardian angel to me ever since.

After four years and three moves, we are now settled on a farm where I am cultivating a new and healthy relationship. I have continued to garden, bake bread, walk and bike for miles, and to live simply.

I feel at times as though my experiences have set me apart and that no one truly understands the meaning of the unique life we led, or, more significantly, what the Ningunsaw Valley meant to me. But finally I enjoy a small network of female friends. I belong to a meditation group and have recently started up a women's reading group. At last I am sharing books.

As for my writing, I have realized my dream and now pursue it full-time. Upon arrival I gave the children a choice between home schooling and public instruction and, craving contact with other kids, they decided to attend public school. Soon after they leave in the morning, I go to my desk.

My book, *Wilderness Mother,* was released in 1994 and was well received, being chosen as a Book-of-the-Month Club selection. My novel, *Ningunsaw,* which went through two readings at McClelland and Stewart and was then turned down, still waits for further work. In 1994, I sold a feature to *Mother Earth News* about returning to civilization and was then invited to do a column for a year. "Shuswap Diary," a series of feature-length stories, appeared from 1994 to 1995. I've pursued such topics as the huge population of bats that inhabited the attic of a nearby church before it burned down, life on a local ostrich farm, and how a female friend built her own adobe house. I've been granted a place on the *Mother Earth News* masthead as contributing editor. I've given readings and for two years I've led workshops at the annual Young Author's Conference at the University College of the Cariboo in Kamloops. And I've now kept journals for twenty-five years. It is impossible to say where my writing path will lead, but that is part of the adventure.

Jay stayed on at our homestead for another two years. Initially he intended to start up a school of self-reliance, but at some point he lost enthusiasm for the idea. In 1994, without discussion, he sold our home and all of the contents to some acquaintances for $10,000. He then returned to Wisconsin, where he helps his mother on her farm and has started up his own market garden business.

The new "owners" paid $1,000, lasted in the bush for eight months, then, upon departure, tried to sell my own home back to me. This began a six-month battle, which would take me another book to fully explain. My story about our only trip back to the Ningunsaw Valley in the spring of 1995 appeared in the October/ November 1995 issue of *Mother Earth News*. There was a happy ending to the dilemma. In October 1995, the B.C. Ministry of Lands decided in our favour and the Ningunsaw homestead officially belongs to Natalia, Ben, and me.

Sometimes when life gets too complicated, I imagine being with Clara and it has a calming effect. And yes, even from afar she has continued to surprise me.

"I bought Clara a three-hundred-piece puzzle some time ago," wrote Fritz in a letter. "At first she couldn't do it and she worked at it for hours. She was getting frustrated, throwing the pieces down. But she stuck to it and finally mastered it, which I thought must have been a real satisfaction. What worries me now is that she is wearing this puzzle out working at it from morning until night."

I remain grateful to Jay for bringing Clara into my life, for show- ing me that love can flow between two vastly different vessels, even though to society, with its shallow version of togetherness, the relationship may remain an enigma.

I believe there were karmic reasons for Fritz and Clara's union. There was a soul more advanced than was evident at first inhabiting Clara's spare frame. Both she and Fritz have learned a great deal by being together. At the same time, Clara showed me that it is possible to be oneself in a relationship and to still be accepted.

Clara cared deeply for others and had her own sense of community. She liked to see people happy. It brought forth a beam from her own weathered countenance. She was better than most of us at remembering people, and after a single meeting their faces became fossilized in her brain.

I saw that communities can teach us to live with people who are very different from us, ones we may not choose to be with. Yet the differences can also be a deep source of creativity and can end up benefiting both beings.

Knowing Clara showed me how friendships can arrive in surprise packages, and how at the outset we see only the wrapping and not what is inside. Clara was a friend like no other I had ever had before, nor ever expect to have again. While some relationships, meaningful at the time, have nearly vanished from my memory, I will never forget her.

When I walked with Clara, during rare moments I felt the spirit of the tribe around us, felt the nomadic flow in which all wonder is held in movement.

What Clara meant to me was an intense challenge, one of the most baffling relationships I had experienced in my forty years. In the beginning I squirmed at the prospect of being in her company. How far I moved beyond that initial impression! The meeting and gradual getting to know her was a window that opened up to a wider and wider view. She was also a mirror for my own shortcomings and limited attitudes. She reflected me back and I learned when I was being dishonest, where I was weak and when I was strong.

Clara showed me how I might alter myself, where to remove some stitches here, to let the hem down there, to loosen the waistline on my robe of personal prejudices, and to let the garment enfold not so much a social outcast as a truly special human being.

Clara meant the presence of a trusted friend, of someone who would stick by me no matter what drudgery I was caught up in, be it physical or emotional. Clara would accept my silence and would happily sit beside me for hours simply sharing the moment while the sky goddess hurled clouds at the mountaintops and the blue grouse built nests near the ancient trails of the grizzly. She meant a pal, a ready hug, a confidante because she absorbed a wide array of thought on our walks through the woods and was incapable of repeating any of it. My ideas must be snagged somewhere in her psychic branches. Perhaps they still sway there like old man's beard lichen in the glacier wind.

From Clara I learned patience, tolerance, and the capacity to stand up for myself more often. She showed me that no matter how uneducated or intellectually stunted we are, somewhere within dwells a spirit with clenched fist and chin held high, which will rise in defence of itself. Call it human dignity or the survival instinct. Without it we won't survive in our full capacity. The soul light can be turned down to a mere flicker by the blackness of oppression. Clara reminded me that I had rights and not to tolerate their violation.

What I learned about communication from Clara was the vital need for all of us to be understood. And that what we all need most apart from basic physical demands is acceptance. And love.

There was a certain freedom that came with discovering her many facets shining through the mentally defective label. With fresh insight I learned that she was every bit as complex as any so-called *normal* human being.

Over time I have come to realize how rare true friendship is. With her elaborately braided hair and her quizzical little smile, Clara was as constant as the north star.

She came to show me the secret that lies hidden in the dense underbrush, overgrown with pain, fear, and sorrow. There nestles an exquisite snail shell. The beauty in each and every soul. Like all life, Clara's was sacred, worthy of honour. Her uniqueness will shine in my mind for the rest of my days.

∞∞∞∞∞

# About the Author

Eric Procunier

Deanna Kawatski was born in Salmon Arm and grew up in the interior of British Columbia. After finishing school, she spent three years abroad before settling in northwestern B.C. She is the author of the best-selling book *Wilderness Mother,* the true story of raising her family on a remote homestead. Her writing has appeared in *Harrowsmith, B.C. Woman to Woman, Canadian Gardening, Outdoor Canada,* and *Country Journal.* She is a contributing editor to *Mother Earth News* as well as one of the magazine's most popular authors. Deanna lives on a farm at Shuswap Lake, B.C., with her daughter and son.